A Bargain With God

The Tony Fontane Story

Charles Randall

Clarion Publishing
Staunton, Virginia

For a man I met
only once.

Table of Contents

Preface

My father repaired cash registers for a living and rarely came home with anything in his hands other than a heavy, black, Samsonite case filled with a bewildering array of tools. But not this evening. This winter's evening in 1964 his other hand held, of all things, a record album. To this day I don't know when, where, or how he came by it – he'd never brought one home before and never did again – but there it was, big as life, and he handed it to me with instructions to safeguard it until after supper (This, by the way, was the South; supper, not dinner, was the evening meal).

As I carefully laid the album in a record caddy beside our floor-model hi-fi unit, I examined the cover. The image of a handsome, raven-haired young man in a tailored dining jacket stared back at me. *Tony Fontane Sings the Songs of Haldor Lillenas*. I shrugged, unimpressed. Who was this guy, anyhow?

When the supper dishes had been cleared and put away, my parents and I trooped into the living room where my mother switched on the hi-fi and got our new record to spinning. From the instant the needle slipped into the vinyl grooves traveling at 33 1/3 revolutions per minute, I was transfixed. The clearest, purest, most electrifying tenor voice I had ever heard filled the room, thrilling me on the high notes and melting my heart on the soft ones. Who was this guy, anyhow?

He was Tony Fontane, my parents explained, a man who had once enjoyed a popular singing career but who, after a near-fatal automobile accident, had given it all up to devote his life and talent to Christ. Already, at the age of twelve, I was beginning to secretly shun the religious teachings of my parents and head down what would become a long path of rebellion and agnosticism, and I couldn't help but wonder why anyone would turn his back on the fame and fortune of a popular career for one as a gospel singer.

But that voice. That incredible, lyric tenor voice. I'd never heard anything like it, and with every song it swept aside my budding hostility toward Christianity and an already well-

1

established disdain of gospel music. Soon, when no one was around, I began playing the record on my own, singing the songs at the top of my lungs, and gaining inspiration from the clarion voice of Tony Fontane.

I played that record until the grooves had grooves.

But over the next few years I traveled a considerable distance down the road of mutiny and discontent, despite the unflagging efforts of my parents to keep me on the straight and narrow. In 1969, as a seventeen-year-old runaway, I ended up in a Schenectady, New York jail; I had already developed a growing dependence upon alcohol and tobacco; and as I ramped up my pursuit of adventure by preparing to join the Marine Corps after high school, I gleefully eliminated God and all the trappings of religion from my life. It was part of an ill-conceived but earnest plan to live as fast as I could, and die as young as I could.

That year, Tony Fontane came to my hometown of Staunton, Virginia, for a series of performances. I remembered the lyric tenor voice that had thrilled me just five years before, and I knew – even though God was no longer on my radar screen – that I had to hear this man perform in person. He sang one evening in the gymnasium of John Lewis Junior High School. I went, and once again marveled at the power, clarity, and expressiveness of his voice.

Afterwards, scores of people surged forward to have him sign album covers, slips of paper, Bibles. I managed to worm my way through the crowd and stand at Fontane's elbow. What to say to him? I'd heard he'd once hobnobbed with Hollywood's elite, so the budding interviewer in me prompted me to ask him about one of my favorite actors.

"I hear you knew Errol Flynn," I said.

"That's right," Fontane replied, still signing autographs.

"What was he like?"

Fontane gave me a sidelong glance and said, "Oh, he was pretty wild."

And that was that. The crowd pressed around him and I moved away, not at all satisfied with my encounter. More than three decades would pass before I would know why.

When I heard in 1974 that Fontane had died, I admittedly gave little thought to the man whose voice had inspired me just a few years earlier. The adventure I'd sought as a teenager was being delivered – in spades – by the Marine Corps, and the years that followed my military tenure were filled with even more colorful and unpublishable experiences. Fontane would not enter my mind again until 2004 when, as a freelance writer, I was casting about for a local history story.

Many notable people have visited Staunton, among them U.S. Presidents, military heroes, sports figures, writers, musicians and movie stars. As I mentally scanned the inventory and debated which celebrity visit would make the best story, Tony Fontane – unbeckoned and quite unexpectedly – sprang to mind. I recall the moment it happened, and how it stopped me dead in my tracks. Tony Fontane, I thought. Now where did he come from?

But the more I reflected on it, the better the idea sounded. Fontane's life story – his rise to stardom, the devastating car crash, his conversion to Christianity, and his untimely death – alone were worth writing about. Moreover, his visit in 1969 had generated modest controversy because he'd sung in several local schools, breaching (in some people's minds) the separation of church and state. Fontane quickly moved to the top of my story list.

The next step, of course, was to research his life. Confident, I started on the Internet and found almost nothing of a biographical nature – just a tidbit here and there. I did find a 1962 movie produced by Gospel Films titled, *The Tony Fontane Story,* and purchased it, but it presented the singer's life in great, broad strokes, and generated more questions than it answered. Still confident, though, I began scouring libraries for lists of periodicals that might have published articles on Fontane, and came up empty-handed. Now bewildered, irritated and not nearly as confident as I had been, I asked myself how someone who had once entertained millions of people through recordings, radio, television shows, and concert appearances, could so completely have dropped out of sight in just thirty years?

I did what any writer worth his salt would do when faced

3

with a brick wall: I broke out a sledgehammer. Although I had only a smattering of information about Fontane, I was convinced of the power of his life's story and decided that it was far too important to tell in a single newspaper article, or even a series of them. I had to write Fontane's biography.

I knew that in order to piece together an accurate portrait of the man, I'd have to talk to the people who'd known and worked with him. This, in itself, posed a problem, because many of Fontane's show business friends and co-workers – among them John Wayne, Ed Sullivan, Steve Allen, Sophie Tucker, Rosemary Clooney, Frank Sinatra, Dean Martin and Sammy Davis Jr. – were dead. When I discovered through the Social Security Death Index that Fontane's wife, Kerry, had passed away in 1996, I knew I had only one more major card to play.

That card was Char'ae Fontane.

Char Fontane – the only child of Tony and Kerry Fontane – first appeared professionally in The Tony Fontane Story, and in the coming years developed an enviably busy television, stage and film career. But all professional credits for her ended in the late 1980s and a phone number provided by the Screen Actors Guild was no longer valid. I checked with the high school from which she'd graduated and came up with nothing. I wrote letters to people with whom she'd appeared in television shows and received not even one response. Finally, in desperation, I looked up all the Char Fontanes or any variation thereof in Internet telephone directories and started making phone calls.

One listing was for a "Shar" Fontane, in Murfreesboro, Tennessee. Despite the inaccurate first-name spelling, I left a message on an answering machine. Days passed. I left more messages on other recorders, got wrong or disconnected numbers the rest of the time. Then, about a week later, a clear, almost musical voice on my home answering machine said, "This is Char Fontane, returning your call."

Not more than thirty seconds later, Tony Fontane's daughter and I were rattling away as though we'd known each other all our lives. And it was during this initial conversation that we both began to sense that my proposed biography of her father was somehow meant to be. Of all the phone numbers I'd called, the one for "Shar" had been the right one. To boot, she said, it was an old number that was going to be disconnected in a week. If my search had taken only a few days longer, I would have missed her entirely.

But there was much more to this sense of inevitability than just a lucky hit with a telephone number. I learned from Char that within the past few months, she had survived a bout with breast cancer.

"I knew I'd been spared for a reason, but I really didn't know what that reason was," she said. "I've done a lot of praying that God would make it clear to me, and I think this is perhaps it. What better way to share with people the message of Christ and what he can do for us than to help tell my father's incredible story?"

Char put me in touch with Fontane's charming and gracious family, who helped provide information that otherwise would have remained inaccessible. Char also suggested the creation of a Web site as a way to gather yet more reminiscences about her father.

However, lest this preface be perceived as simply a chronicle of how I came to write Tony Fontane's biography, let me stress that uncovering many of the details of his life was less a researcher's success than it was a triumph of God over some very persistent worldly obstacles – not the least of which was my own idiocy. For now, many years after crowding in at Tony Fontane's elbow and asking him stupid questions about dead movie stars, I realize what an opportunity had presented itself and how I'd let it get away. Now I know why my fleeting contact with him was so unsatisfactory. I'd asked the wrong question about the wrong person. So now – more than forty years after seeing the handsome young man on the album cover and being swept up by his voice – I am endeavoring to answer the right question, the one I asked from that very first day:

Who was this guy, anyhow?

Chapter One

Tony Fontane emerged from a rehearsal at NBC's production studio in Burbank, California, and squinted against the glare of a brilliant September afternoon. Donning a pair of sunglasses, the thirty-one-year-old pop singer made his way across the parking lot toward his new 1957 Mercedes-Benz 300 SL. A voice drew him up as he opened the door of the car.

"Good work, Tony," said his agent. "This is going to be a great television special. I think it's really going to get you some traction."

"Thanks," Fontane said with a grin. "Let's just keep it going, okay?"

He slid under the wheel of the Mercedes, fired up the engine, and wheeled out of the parking lot. Making his way to Balboa Boulevard and heading north towards his Canoga Park home, Fontane centered his thoughts on his schedule for the next few months. Television appearances, recording sessions, radio shows, and Las Vegas night club bookings. The clear tenor voice that had materialized from out of nowhere just after World War II was still in demand, and Fontane sensed that his career was moving up to a new level. And he very much needed that to happen. Although he was busy, and fully booked, and making more money than he could spend, he hadn't had a Top Ten hit in the United States since 1951, six years earlier. Fontane yearned for greater success, and he intended to have it at almost any cost.

Fontane smiled grimly. Almost any cost. There was one price he hadn't paid. He had achieved it all without even once calling upon the God of his parents – the God he hated, the God that had made his early life miserable, the God he didn't believe existed. He, Anthony Trankina – now popular as Tony Fontane – was responsible for the successes that had come his way. Natural ability and a single-minded determination had allowed him to carve out a lucrative niche in the entertainment industry. God? God was a fiction, he thought, and a cruel one at that.

The smile dropped from Fontane's lips as he continued his journey through the San Fernando Valley. A strange foreboding always descended upon him whenever his thoughts turned to God, life, success, and how they connected with one another. Reflexively, he conducted the mental inventory that always reaffirmed his belief in his own happiness: money in the bank, recording contract, public appearances, fast cars, expensive home, beautiful wife and daughter. He numbered among his friends some of the biggest names in Hollywood. The largest, most prestigious booking agency in the world, William Morris, represented him. What more could a man in the prime of his life and career ask for?

And yet, no matter how often or doggedly he validated his life in these terms, Fontane couldn't quite shake the sense of emptiness and discontent that had plagued him for years. He refused to concede, or to even consider, that anything other than external forces were responsible for the successes that fell to him in life. If he felt unfulfilled in any way, surely a new record album, television show, or Las Vegas appearance could fix it. After all, he – Tony Fontane and no one else – was in charge of his life and was responsible for the quality of its content.

Still immersed in these thoughts, he brought the Mercedes to a halt at the intersection of Balboa Boulevard and Sherman Way. Signaling a left turn onto Sherman, Fontane waited for the light to change to green. When it did, he nudged the Mercedes forward and quickly gained the heart of the intersection. For the merest fraction of a second he was aware of an object hurtling toward the driver's side of his car. And then the world went dark.

Five-year-old Char'ae Fontane spent the afternoon of September 3, 1957, as she frequently did, playing at the Kelvin Avenue home of her best friend, Sharon Mason. The Mason home stood just five doors down from the Fontane residence, and on this bright, warm California afternoon the two little girls squealed and danced through the showers of a lawn sprinkler, oblivious to anything more serious than an occasional squabble with a neighborhood boy.

Life may have been more carefree and adventurous for

8

Char'ae – Char to all who knew her – than for many of her contemporaries. Her father was a well-liked recording and night club singer and her mother a former dancer and film actress. Some of Char's earliest memories included traveling with her glamorous parents to Australia where her parents performed in the musical comedy, Zip Goes A Million, and where her mother's great beauty gained her widespread billing as a second Marilyn Monroe. The glittering lifestyle of Tony and Kerry Fontane brought to Char all the amenities that money could buy, and her parents' unusually stable Hollywood relationship gave her the love and security she needed. Like most children, she took it for granted, and thought it would last forever.

Most of it would last for only another few minutes.

Kay Mason, Sharon's mother, was a brusque, no-nonsense Australian who seldom minced words, even when the situation called for it. It had been Mrs. Mason's bluntness that, just the year before, had destroyed the illusion of Santa Claus for four-year-old Char. As September 3, 1957 stretched into late afternoon and Char and Sharon continued to play under the sprinkler, Mrs. Mason received a telephone call. Hanging up the phone a few moments later, she walked out of her house and pulled Char aside.

"Your father's been in a car wreck," she said brusquely. "He's probably going to die."

Char stood transfixed for a moment, unable to move or speak. Then she began to cry, and a scream leapt from her throat. She broke away from the Masons and raced down the sidewalk to her home. Bursting through the front door, Char found her mother in a near-hysterical condition, but trying with the help of several neighbors to collect herself for a drive to the hospital.

"There's no way he could survive this," Char heard one neighbor tell Kerry Vaughn Fontane. "You've got to prepare yourself."

Kay Mason appeared and began to talk about funeral arrangements, and again Char broke into tears. How could this happen, she thought? This was her beloved father they were talking about – her smiling, indulgent, indestructible father –

and her father couldn't just die like that. Then she looked at her mother's tear-streaked face, and the grim visages of the neighbors who were helping ready her for a trip to the hospital, and thought: Or could he?

Fifty-six-year-old Lester Franklin Carson of 7740 Balboa Boulevard was headed west on Sherman Way when he failed to stop for the light at Sherman and Balboa. As Tony Fontane entered the intersection, Carson slammed into the driver's side of the Mercedes and left it a smoking, twisted pile of metal. Pedestrians raced to Fontane's aid and tried to open his door, but the impact of the collision had jammed it shut. Meanwhile, inside, an unconscious Fontane began to bleed from scores of injuries. Carson was unhurt.

Within minutes the intersection teemed with police officers, medical personnel and rescue workers. While police tackled the traffic that was backing up in all directions, paramedics tried to pry open the doors of the Mercedes. The violence of the crash, however, had wedged both doors tightly shut, and the sports car's fragile internal structure had twisted and crumpled to form a barrier around Fontane. He was, literally, sealed in a vehicle that rapidly was becoming his coffin.

Even though rescue workers attacked the car with acetylene torches and cut away the passenger door, minutes turned into half-hours, and half-hours into hours as they labored to free the singer. Once the door was removed, rescuers had to carefully pry enough metal away from Fontane to gingerly pull him from the Mercedes. When they finally did, after two-and-a-half hours, even the most experienced paramedic winced at the extent of his injuries. Drenched in blood, Fontane looked like he had passed through a barbed-wire fence.

A paramedic picked up his wrist and checked his pulse. He shook his head.

"He's dead."

"Wait a minute," said another paramedic, placing a stethoscope against Fontane's mangled chest. He paused, listened, and said, "I hear something. Very faint. Let's get him out of here. Now!"

Fontane was moved onto a stretcher and placed into a waiting ambulance. With siren wailing, the ambulance raced toward Northridge Receiving Hospital on Sherman Way. Radioing ahead, the ambulance crew told dispatchers at Northridge that the victim was severely injured with, at the minimum, head, hip and chest fractures. They didn't comment on his chances for recovery, but no one who loaded Tony Fontane into the ambulance that day believed they were delivering anything other than a dead man to the emergency room.

Doctors at Northridge quickly came to the same conclusion. Fontane, they discovered, had massive internal injuries, a fractured skull, a brain concussion, a number of dislocated vertebrae, and seven broken ribs. Both of his legs had been broken above the knee. His chest had been crushed. He had lost copious quantities of blood. Unconscious and hanging onto life by the merest of threads, he breathed at the behest of a ventilator and lay quietly thanks only to a steady drip of morphine. Fontane, it was decided, had only minutes, hours at best, to live.

At about the time Fontane was wheeled into emergency surgery to the relieve pressure on his brain, repair his chest, set his legs, and stabilize his many other wounds, a distraught Kerry Fontane arrived at the hospital. Her finely chiseled features were streaked with tears as she watched her husband, who was oblivious to his surroundings, being taken away for surgery. A doctor drew her aside and warned her that she may not see him alive again.

"His wounds are many and deep," said the doctor. "It's a miracle he's made it even this far. I'm telling you this because I think you should know the score, Mrs. Fontane."

Grim-faced, Kerry Fontane dug into the depths of her purse and took out a checkbook. Tearing off a blank check, she held it out to the doctor.

"Fill it out for any amount you need," she said. "Just save Tony's life."

The doctor shook his head. "There isn't enough money in the world to enable us to do anything for your husband," he said. "He's in God's hands, now."

Fifteen hundred miles to the northeast, in Grand Forks, North Dakota, the Reverend Joseph Trankina leaned into his pulpit and began the evening sermon. Seated before him in the chapel of the Grand Forks Rescue Mission and Service Center was a sampling of the area's least fortunate citizens – the hungry, homeless, downtrodden and despairing; alcoholics, wanderers, outcasts and derelicts – the kind of men and women Trankina had spent a large portion of his life trying to help. This small chapel with its humble altar and folding chairs formed the cornerstone of the mission he and his late wife, Raphaela, had founded in 1942 as a way to feed, clothe and minister to those who needed it.

The Trankinas had raised their four children in an atmosphere of Christian service to humanity. All had been exposed to Trankina's staunch devotion to helping the materially and spiritually less fortunate in life, and to his wife's quiet, loving, and solid fidelity to the principles laid out in the Bible. Of their four children, only one had turned his back on the teachings of his parents. Only one had refused to yield to the Biblical lessons learned at his mother's knee. Only one had developed a hatred for all things religious. Tony, the child with the high, clear tenor voice, set off into the world with a stage name – Fontane – and a burning desire to put as much distance as he could between himself and the austerity of life at the North Dakota mission.

The Reverend Trankina's only daughter, Nina, worked as a registered nurse at the Grand Forks Hospital, and regularly volunteered at the mission to help her father with daily operations. This chilly September night, she stationed herself near the front of the chapel and settled in to hear her father preach the Word of God. Trankina had been speaking for only a few minutes when the telephone in the mission office began to ring. Nina, not wanting the service to be disrupted, quickly made her way to the office and picked up the receiver. On the other end of the line was a shattered Kerry Fontane.

Nina's heart began to fill with dread as she learned of her brother's horrific automobile accident, and of his next-to-zero chances for survival. Kerry, who was calling from Fontane's

12

bedside in the critical care unit of Northridge Receiving, asked Nina to tell the Reverend Trankina the news.

"Dad's in a service, but I'll go get him right now," Nina said. "Hang on."

Nina hurried back into the chapel and signaled to her father.

"It's an urgent phone call," she said.

The Reverend Trankina motioned for a mission volunteer to take over the sermon, and dashed into the office near the front of the chapel. He picked up the telephone, and listened with a sinking heart as Kerry told him the grim news. Trankina dropped into a chair and said he would try to get on a plane as soon as possible, and then spent many minutes trying to soothe the deeply troubled Kerry.

"When Tony was born," Trankina told Kerry, "his mother and I dedicated him to the Lord. So, I know God is in control, even during this serious, life-threatening situation."

After praying with Kerry, Trankina asked, "Will you put the phone to Tony's ear so that I may pray with him, even though he can't hear me?"

Kerry did, and from fifteen hundred miles away, Trankina spoke into his unconscious son's ear, and prayed that he would do two things: survive, and give his heart to God. Afterward, he spoke with Kerry again and told her of God's love for her, and that she, too, should consider giving her heart to the Lord.

Trankina went back into the chapel, and from the pulpit told the congregation what had happened. Tearfully, the transients and indigents in the mission chapel began to pray for a man most knew only by reputation. To a person, they prayed for God to spare his life.

"That night," Nina said years later, "my Dad couldn't sleep. He prayed all night."

Thirty days later, Tony Fontane still had not regained consciousness. Transferred from Northridge's emergency department to the critical care unit of Angels' Hospital, the singer lay in a deep coma, his every breath anticipated by doctors to be his last. Kerry left Char'ae in the care of neighbors and spent all day, every day at the hospital. She, like her husband, was not a religious person and, by extension, did not pray. But she sat by Fontane's bedside day after day, held his hand, talked to him, stroked his cheek, and hoped against hope that he would somehow return to her. They had been married for only seven and a half years, and Kerry – who had seen firsthand the toll that the entertainment industry took on marriages – jealously held onto this happy union with her talented, volatile, headstrong husband. She simply refused to believe that this was the end.

At home in the evenings, Kerry made an effort to remain upbeat for Char, who wasn't allowed to visit her father in the hospital. Every night Char would ask how her father was, and every night Kerry would say, "He's going to be all right." But the strain took its toll. One night, Kerry came home and collapsed into tears.

"I don't think he is going to be all right," she admitted to Char, who followed suit with a flood of tears of her own.

Indeed, the situation was bleak. Fontane's doctors had managed, so far, to keep him alive, a fact that frankly astonished them. Rarely had they seen a patient survive with such massive internal and external injuries or, if they did survive, return to any kind of normal, useful life. And they were honest with Kerry about it.

"We don't think he's going to make it, Mrs. Fontane," a physician told her. "If he does, well...You may not want him to. He will most likely be dependent on you for everything for the rest of his life."

"You mean he's going to be a vegetable?" she asked.

"Unfortunately, yes," the doctor replied.

In early October, after Fontane had remained comatose for a full month, his eyes fluttered open. A quick series of tests revealed that swelling of the brain had rendered him blind, and he couldn't speak; but he was alive, and apparently he wasn't the vegetable his doctors had predicted he would be. Lying in his hospital bed, fed intravenously, still hovering on the fringe of consciousness, Fontane was aware of the activity around him and of his wife's presence.

His thoughts, as he later noted in a magazine interview, were not of his singing voice or his career, but of his very life and whether or not he would be able to continue it.

The situation remained grim into the fall of 1957, with Fontane's doctors still holding out little hope for his recovery. One day, at two o'clock in the morning, the singer plunged back into unconsciousness and his vital signs plummeted, indicating that the end was, at last, near. A staff consultation confirmed it. This time they were sure. Tony Fontane had only hours to live, and a telephone call was placed to his wife. Kerry quickly left Char in the care of a neighbor and hurried to the hospital.

Like her husband, Kerry Vaughn had received a Christian upbringing. Unlike her husband, however, she was not an atheist. In her pursuit of a film career at Metro Goldwyn Mayer and Universal Studios, she had had no time for things religious and had allowed herself to slip into a secular way of thinking and living. But during her marriage to Fontane she had met and talked at length with his mother, Raphaela Trankina. Now, as Kerry entered her husband's hospital room for what would most likely be the last time, she recalled the quiet but earnest Christian testimony of Fontane's mother.

Kerry approached Fontane's bed, looked down at the dying man, and slowly dropped to her knees. She began to pray.

"Lord," she said, "here and now I accept you as my savior. I don't know how I'll do it – you'll have to show me – but I promise that I will spend the rest of my life serving you. Let Tony live so that we can serve you together."

She continued to pray for the next three and a half hours.

Darkness enveloped him like a warm, heavy blanket. For the first time in recent memory he was no longer in pain. He had the sensation of drifting further and further downward into an irresistible black calm. He no longer heard the sounds in his room. He no longer felt the tubes and the bandages and the crisp sheets of his hospital bed. He was slipping away and he knew it. And he no longer cared.

All at once a single, hot point of light appeared in the center of the darkness. It grew, imperceptibly at first, then mushroomed with increasing speed until the warm, gooey blackness retreated to the outer periphery of his awareness. And then he saw it. A form, materializing at the core of the light. It was indistinct, with no recognizable facial features or physical characteristics, but it was a figure nonetheless. It moved toward him, connected with him, enshrouded him with a feeling of calm and contentment that he had never known and had never realized could exist.

The figure, he knew, was Jesus. Jesus had come for him. It was time to go.

But then the figure of Christ began to speak, not with the voice of a man, with vocal chords, but with thoughts, transmitting them directly into Fontane's mind. And what he said was not what Fontane expected.

"I am going to give you a second chance."

Fontane responded, likewise with his thoughts.

"A second chance? You're going to let me live?"

"Yes. I am going to give you a second chance, Tony, and I want you to dedicate your life to me. Will you do it?"

Fontane, at peace for the first time in his life, said yes, and even as his coma held him in its grip, accepted Christ as his savior. As he did, the figure of Jesus gradually receded into the light, and the light gave way once more to the darkness. But Fontane watched them go without alarm and without fear, for he knew his soul was safe and that his life was coming back to him.

After three and a half hours of prayer, Kerry Fontane struggled up from her husband's bedside and gazed down at the comatose man. Had her prayers worked, or had they been in vain? Was prayer, she asked herself, an overrated, religious panacea with no real power or effect in a harsh and unforgiving world? No. She couldn't and wouldn't think that way. God, she knew from her childhood lessons, did not lie, and would not consign her prayers to oblivion without just cause. She would trust, hope, and pray some more.

Her heart nearly leapt out of her chest. For an instant she

thought she had seen movement in the bed. Stepping closer to Fontane, she watched him with a fierce intensity. Yes! There it was again! His eyes fluttered, and a low moan eased out of his throat. Instinctively she glanced around for a doctor or a nurse, but realized that she and Fontane were alone. Unwilling to leave his side, she reached out and placed her hand on his forehead. And that's when his eyes popped open.

"Kerry," he croaked, a grin spreading across his boyish face. "Kerry, I just had the most amazing dream."

Kerry, tears forming in her eyes, reached out and took his hand. "Yes, Tony?"

"I dreamed that Jesus came to me, and talked to me, and said he'd give me another chance, and I agreed to give my life to him," he said, rattling off the words as glibly as if his coma had never existed.

It was then that Kerry told Fontane of her three-and-a-half-hour prayer vigil, and of her acceptance of Christ. Together, now, they prayed again, with Fontane verbally asking Jesus to come into his life and his soul. Together, they wept, and together they faced an uncertain future in which there would be only one constant – God.

That night, while Tony Fontane slept, Kerry telephoned his father and sister in Grand Forks. She told them that not only was he going to live, but that he – and she – had given their lives to God.

"Dad and I were so happy we wanted to jump for joy," said Fontane's sister, Nina. "Dad couldn't sleep that night, either. He prayed all night thanking God."

Chapter Two

It was a curious image for a gospel singer to have. On the one hand, Tony Fontane presented the quintessential picture of a man who had given his life and his talents to God. He had, after all, turned his back on a lucrative popular career to record and perform gospel music only, an admirable trait when one considered the fruits a secular entertainment career could provide. On the other hand, Fontane's elegance and style led some to mistakenly believe that his emphasis was on earthly riches rather than heavenly rewards. The tuxedos, the highly touted albums, the cars, the seemingly glamorous touring schedule, and the women – lots of them, in fact – who wanted firsthand knowledge of his ability to either withstand physical temptation or to succumb to it, projected to some the image of a man enjoying all the world had to offer through the good graces of the Christian music industry.

While one of the mainstays of Fontane's career as a gospel singer was the story of the ghastly automobile accident that nearly killed him, the public at large possessed no inkling of the enormous challenges that had faced Tony Fontane throughout his life, not the least of which had occurred in the aftermath of the wreck. Had they known, they might have passed fewer judgments on his choice of lifestyle or, rather, the lifestyle they thought he lived, and appreciated more the music and message he brought to millions through his concerts and recordings.

It all started in Chicago at the turn of the twentieth century, where the promise of labor lured millions of immigrants from nearly every corner of the world. In what was perhaps the single greatest melting pot in a nation known for its assimilation of different peoples, Swedish, Irish, Polish, Russian, and Jewish immigrants knocked out a hardscrabble existence in close-knit enclaves throughout the city. And between 1880 and 1920, more than four million Italians, streaming through New York's Ellis Island to escape the grinding poverty and lack of opportunity of their native land, descended upon the Windy City with their eyes firmly focused on the American Dream.

It was into this volatile mix of races, creeds, cultures, and dreams that Joseph Vincent Trankina was born on April 22, 1904, the son of Sicilian immigrants. Almost from the outset it seemed that the world was against him. While he was still a youngster, Trankina lost his mother when she died at age thirty-seven from complications of childbirth. Soon after that, Trankina's father died of an inoperable heart tumor at the age of thirty-eight. While he was sometimes shunted off to various family members, young Joe Trankina was essentially on his own in a very tough city. He slept in doorways. He huddled in alleys at night against the bitter Chicago winter winds. And, inevitably, he had to fight for his life against street toughs who were bigger, stronger, and more vicious than he was. But rather than weakening him, the experiences toughened him, and by the age of eleven he had shown such skill with his bare knuckles that he started boxing in one of the city's slum-side gymnasiums.

Wiry, agile and hard as hickory, Joe Trankina began to make a name for himself as a boxer, first in amateur bouts and then for prize money. His was a no-nonsense, no-frills existence, and his outlook on life was as hard as the fists that plowed out his living for him. And while he had been born and raised in a Roman Catholic family – his mother had made him promise that he would one day meet her in heaven – religion played no part in his life. It was, in fact, the last thing on his mind. Survival and survival only was the linchpin of Trankina's life, with some drinking and gambling thrown in for good measure. God, for Joe Trankina, simply didn't exist.

In 1921, at the age of seventeen, Trankina visited Hull House at the corner of Polk and Halsted streets. The house, which was opened to the public as a gathering place for immigrants and the poor by Jane Addams in 1889, was also a popular gathering place for young people. It was here that Trankina came face to face with the most beautiful young woman he had ever seen. Their eyes locked. The attraction was mutual and instantaneous. The street-wise young boxer had no trouble introducing himself to Raphaela Galluzzi, but Raphaela – Rae, as she was known – hailed from a quality family that had high hopes for this dark

Italian beauty. They did not consider Joe Trankina, prize fighter, as part of that future. They forbade Rae to see him or to even speak to him, which only increased Trankina's determination to court her. And he did.

During this time, the refined, soft-spoken Rae told Trankina that she objected to his career in the ring, that it wasn't a suitable profession for an up-and-coming family man. Acquiescing to her wishes, Trankina retired from boxing and took a job with a railroad construction company. When he and Rae were married on November 4, 1922, Trankina applied for, and got, a job with the Michigan Central Railroad. He and his new wife then took in Trankina's youngest brother, Leonard, who also had been passed from one relative to another after the deaths of their parents, and raised him as their own child.

With a wife, a job and responsibilities now taking center stage, Trankina made a sincere effort to turn his life around. He worked hard and soon began to move up in the railroad hierarchy, gaining the position of head time keeper and finally that of general supervisor of two hundred and fifty railroad construction men. But it still wasn't an easy life. He and his young wife were compelled to move from place to place as dictated by the needs of the Michigan Central, and the easiest most convenient lodging during this time was a railroad boxcar. No plumbing, no electricity, no heat, no amenities of any kind. Just a boxcar for three people, soon to be four, for Rae was pregnant with their first child.

That first child, Vincent Trankina, was born in 1923 while the family was stationed in Chicago. Two years later, on September 18, 1925, another son was born in the boxcar, which now was parked on the Michigan Central's tracks in Ann Arbor, Michigan. They named the new baby Anthony, but forever after would refer to him as Tony.

Life in a boxcar, particularly in the middle of Michigan and Illinois winters, was austere in the extreme. Cooking and washing were difficult enough, but toiletry and privacy were even harder to achieve. Trankina, accustomed from an early age to discomfort, probably adjusted the quickest, but his gentle

Raphaela, who had led a privileged life as a girl, never faltered and never complained. She took over housekeeping and child-rearing duties gracefully, never once complaining about her lot in life or regretting her marriage to Joe Trankina.

Even though she had defied her family by marrying him, and even though their living conditions were many levels below the one she had grown up with, Rae had not been completely abandoned by her family. Her mother, Rosalie, often visited them at their home on the tracks and would bring with her a three-year-old granddaughter. Visiting Uncle Joe and Aunt Rae in their boxcar was always a treat for the girl, who frequently begged her grandmother to take her for a visit.

One day, on just such a visit when the Trankinas were back in Chicago, the grandmother and child were outside the Trankina boxcar when two railroad workers, operating in a drunken fog, unwittingly unhooked a caboose and allowed it to lurch onto an unauthorized track. At the end of that track was the boxcar home of Joe and Rae Trankina.

The caboose careened down an incline straight for the boxcar. Outside, grandmother Rosalie and her granddaughter were playing on the tracks, oblivious to the danger barreling straight for them. When they finally did realize what was happening, it was too late. They tried to escape, but the wheels of the runaway caboose caught the hem of the little girl's dress and yanked her under the car. She was nearly decapitated.

Unfathomable anguish filled the Trankina home. Rae and her mother were inconsolable. When Joe found out that the engineer and brakeman responsible for the runaway caboose had been drunk, he was filled with a murderous rage. It was on that day, his daughter said many years later, that he "turned against God completely."

"He said that a loving God would not let this happen," she recalled in 2002.

Trankina's thoughts turned to violence. The men who had done this, he reasoned, must die. Arming himself with a pistol and a knife, he set out into the railroad yard to look for the engineer and brakeman. He hadn't gone far when a railroad

22

official, probably suspecting that the hot-blooded Trankina would seek revenge, intercepted him and convinced him that the slaying of the men would solve nothing. Pleading with him to think of his wife and children, the official finally got Trankina to hand over his weapons and go home.

A few days later, after the little girl's funeral, Trankina returned to work to find that a new inspector had been hired. Since Trankina was a supervisor, he'd have to work closely with the new man. Almost immediately the new man began to talk about God, to which the still hurting Trankina promptly replied, "There is no God." The new inspector began to quiz him, asking Trankina why he was an atheist, and reading to him from the New Testament. Trankina, despite his arrogance and anger, found himself listening to the inspector rather than arguing with him.

During one of their conversations in the railroad yard one day, Trankina began to feel his cold-heartedness and skepticism slipping away from him. Together he and the inspector knelt down, with the railroad tracks their altar, and accepted Christ as his savior. When he got back on his feet, he was not the same Joe Trankina who had knelt there a few moments earlier. It was as if a smoky film had been stripped from his eyes, and he could see clearly for the first time in his life. His soul, formerly calloused and heavy with the weight of sin and care, now felt as light as gossamer. It was a changed man who made his way back to the boxcar that evening.

The change was immediately noticeable. Rae's once tough, profane husband was now a calm and compassionate man, possessed of an inner tranquility he had never exhibited before. When he explained what had happened to him, Rae couldn't understand it. Nothing in her Roman Catholic upbringing had prepared her for the kind of epiphany that her husband had just experienced. But she didn't discount it. Quietly, she watched as the change took an ever stronger hold on her husband, until at last she knew that this was neither a fluke nor a fancy. A year later, when Trankina began to talk of finding ways to serve God,

Rae opened her own heart to Christ and joined her husband in a quest to serve their newfound Lord.

Trankina's first step in that direction was to quit his job with the Michigan Central, a risky move considering the railroad provided the family with an income of about seventy-five dollars a month. In 1930, when the Great Depression was just getting under way and jobs were hard to find, Trankina's move reflected courage and an unflagging faith that what he was doing was God's will.

He enrolled in classes at the Moody Bible Institute in Chicago and by night studied the Bible. By day, he and his seven-year-old son, Vince, would take the family's Ford truck and fill it with produce. They would travel down the alleys of Chicago yelling, "Joe's produce," and people would appear on their back porches to place their orders. Trankina would weigh it and Vince would run it to the customer who, sometimes, lived on the third or fourth floor of the tenements.

On weekends, Trankina and Vince would take all the fixtures out of the back of the Ford, hose it down, and put side boards on it so that it would hold a load of coal. Getting up early, they would drive to Lemoyne, Illinois, to a coal mine, purchase a load of lignite which they transferred to the truck by hand, and then sell the slow-burning lignite in Chicago's neighborhoods for fifty cents a bushel.

It was at about this time that Trankina began to conduct street meetings in Chicago, using the back of the Ford as his pulpit. He and Vince would clean and hose down the truck after a day's labor in the produce business, and scoop up a following of people from surrounding churches. Loading a portable, folding organ into the truck, Trankina, Rae and the family would find the busiest street corner in Chicago and hold Bible meetings. Frequently they were pelted with tomatoes and eggs by rowdies who wanted to disrupt the services. Occasionally it worked. While Trankina himself was fearless, he sometimes had to break up the meetings for the safety of the crowd. But he and his family always came back and had another go at leading people to Christ, despite the dangers.

But opposition from street hooligans wasn't the only battle the Trankinas had to face. Joe and Rae, hailing from traditional Italian families, had started their lives following the Roman Catholic faith. When they left their family's traditional Catholic practice to follow an approach to Christ they found more spiritually alive for them, the families threatened to turn their backs on them. There were times when family members lined up on either side of the street to spit upon the couple and verbally insult them for what was perceived as spiritual betrayal. Still they refused to waver, and grew even stronger in their Christianity.

Young Tony Trankina's psyche was seared with these incidents, and not in a positive way. He was, after all, a five-year-old boy who, on a regular basis, had missiles thrown at him by street thugs, and whose parents were shunned by some of their own kin. In his juvenile mind it wasn't the rowdies who were responsible for the humiliation he felt, or the family members who made him an outcast; it was God and the message of salvation his family insisted on preaching that were to blame. While he may still have been too young to form a calculated acceptance of atheism, the emotional foundation for it no doubt was laid on violent Chicago street corners and at the hands of religiously entrenched relatives.

However, the street ministry of Joe Trankina also provided positive lessons for his family. The side of the truck bore his name, "J.V. Trankina," a fact that generated more than a little embarrassment to a rich cousin with the same initials. Jim Trankina, the cousin, chaffed when people constantly told him that they had seen one of his trucks at the street meetings, which he vehemently denied. Finally, he approached Joe Trankina and insisted that he take his name off the truck so as to avoid embarrassing him further. Trankina refused. The cousin then tried to buy him off, offering Trankina a job that paid five thousand dollars a month if he would give up his faith in Christ and stop the street meetings.

Trankina thought about it. This was the Great Depression and sixty thousand dollars a year was more money than he or any of his acquaintances could imagine. But he remembered what his life had been like before he accepted Christ, remembered the violence, the heavy drinking and the gambling.

"All the money in the world can't do what Christ did for me," he told his cousin, and refused the money.

It was, he said later, simply a matter of obeying God rather than man, and it was a lesson he tried to pass on to Leonard, Vince and young Tony.

The lesson taught itself, really. Some two years later, the cousin called Joe and asked him to come to his house and tell his entire family, all thirteen of them, about Jesus and his power to save. Trankina's steadfast, faithful example had led to a unique opportunity to spread the Word of God, an opportunity he took advantage of with great joy.

Trankina's studies at the Moody Bible Institute and other Christian schools in the area threw him together with a variety of people with similar interests, among them Christians who had performed missionary work in various parts of the world. It wasn't long before he began to hear about an increasing need for missions and mission work in frigid Cando, North Dakota, ministering to Indians on the reservations, farmers, derelicts, alcoholics and starving migrants. After a great deal of prayer, he and Rae decided to answer God's call to go to North Dakota.

In February of 1935, Trankina, who had been ordained a Baptist minister in 1932, loaded his family into a 1929 Ford Stake truck – the flatbed vehicle was equipped with stakes on the sides over which a tarpaulin could be stretched – and headed for the wilds of North Dakota. Joe, Rae, and their new arrivals Nina and Joe Jr. rode in the cab, while Tony and Vince rode in the tarpaulin-covered back with the few sticks of furniture the family owned. A small kerosene heater kept the boys from freezing.

Near Minneapolis, the Ford Stake began to sputter and lurch, so Trankina made arrangements to send Rae and the twins ahead to Cando while he, Vince and Tony continued the voyage with the recalcitrant flatbed. Near Jamestown, North Dakota, the radiator sprung a leak, forcing the trip to come to a temporary halt. The trio, now stranded in the North Dakota countryside, approached a farmhouse to get water for the radiator. From inside the house they heard the unmistakable sounds of a terrific battle between the farmer and his wife. Trankina's fist hesitated over the door, but the need for water for the radiator gave him the impetus to knock.

A woman opened the door, her face streaked with tears. She asked Trankina and his sons to come in, which they willingly did. The husband, exhibiting more than a little suspicion of the trio that turned up on his doorstep in the middle of nowhere, was full of questions that Trankina was happy to answer, and to lace with Christian testimony. That night, the farmer and his wife knelt with Trankina and his sons and accepted Christ as their savior. Although Trankina was stranded in the wilds of North Dakota with a broken down truck and two young boys, with little money and a long journey ahead of them, he looked on this incident as a victory and a bright spot in their lives. God, he knew, was at work.

With water in the radiator, Joe, Vince and Tony set off again for Cando, but the Ford died once more. They managed to get the vehicle into Buchanon where they took it to a garage. Here, the garage owner told them the vehicle was finished without a major repair job. Trankina, who was nearly penniless, was honest with the mechanic, and offered to leave his watch for security if the man would fix the truck. He then promised to send the money for the repairs as soon as possible. The garage owner agreed.

Of course, Joe Trankina wasn't about to let a new acquaintance get away without some mention of salvation passing between them. As he witnessed to the owner, several people overheard him and asked him if he would come to one of the homes in the area and preach a sermon. He did, with Vince and Tony in tow, and the result was several North Dakota farmers giving their lives to Christ.

The truck was fixed by the next morning. Trankina handed the garage owner his watch and headed off for Cando. Later, he sent the owner what he owed him – ten dollars – and the garage owner returned the watch, impressed that Trankina had kept his word.

February in North Dakota isn't much of a laughing matter, and when Trankina and his sons arrived in Cando just ninety miles below the Canadian border, the temperature hovered at a painful fifty-one degrees below zero. The building that had been set aside for the new missionary family from Chicago was an old wooden storefront near the railroad tracks that had been divided into two rooms. One room, which measured about fifteen feet by twenty feet, was used for living quarters, and the other, which measured a scant eight feet by fifteen feet, saw service as the family's kitchen. A single stovepipe chimney provided the building's only source of heat. As a purchase against the cold, Rae would heat water on the wood stove downstairs, put it in a Mason jar, and then take it up to the attic where Vince and Tony slept, and would roll it over the sheets to help warm them.

The children walked to school in this brittle climate, often facing blizzards on their way to and from the schoolhouse. To make matters worse, the Trankina boys often had to defend themselves against ethnic-based aggression. Years later, Tony would tell his daughter of having to fistfight his way home from school every day.

"My father came home battered and bruised every single day, but it hardened him quite a bit and gave him a hair-trigger temper. He grew up hard as nails."

And so it was into this frozen, hostile environment that Joe and Rae Trankina made their new home, determined to warm it with the love of God and service to humanity. But as they settled in to launch their ministry, one of their children began to chafe, and to grow resentful, and to burn with an abhorrence of their lifestyle that would soon mature into a ferocious hatred.

He was only nine, but Tony Trankina already knew he wanted out.

Chapter Three

What causes one child in a family to travel a radically different path than his or her siblings, all of whom have had essentially the same upbringing? The only point psychologists agree on is that hundreds of factors come into play, among them genetics, environmental influences, and differences in the way parents rear individual children. Even Tony Trankina, exploring the topic many years later as Tony Fontane, couldn't pinpoint why his sister and brothers all embraced the Christian teachings of their parents while he did not. All he could say with certainty was that he developed a blistering hatred for those teachings, coupled with an equally intense revulsion for the grinding poverty upon which their daily lives were centered. In his young mind, the two elements were inextricably entwined. Because his parents followed Christ and ministered to the outcast, he and the entire family were consigned to a life of privation. Even though Tony had already begun to doubt the existence of God, he had no doubt that God – or rather, his parents' belief in such a being – was to blame for his misery.

The boy's loathing for life within the confines of the mission was reinforced on a daily basis. Every unwashed, drunken, shoeless derelict that came through the mission's doors filled the boy with disgust. Tony, like all the older children, frequently was enlisted to help physically bring drunks into the mission and clean them up. He reviled this chore and, over time, stored up a deep wellspring of anger against the kind of life he was forced to live. One day, he watched in utter disbelief as his father, himself wearing secondhand clothes, took off his shoes and gave them to a transient in need. His mother did the same with a pair of stockings. When Tony had to give up his own shoes for the children of needy couples, his rage and disgust reached new heights.

"At evening services I often heard my father tell the men that God would provide for them if they would just abandon themselves to Him," Tony wrote years later. "It seemed to me that my parents had certainly abandoned themselves to God, and I saw little evidence that He was providing very much."

29

The Reverend Trankina would joke that the family never missed a meal – that they just postponed a lot of them.

"To me," continued Tony, "this was no joke. Nor was the lack of any gifts at birthdays and Christmas. I blamed religion for this."

The Trankinas were aware of the wrath their second-oldest child was harboring, and worked hard to help him overcome it. According to Nina Trankina, Joe and Rae involved him in family projects, played with him, tried to reason with him. They prayed daily for him.

"He was just a strong personality," she recalled. "Anyone with several children in the family usually experiences the same thing."

Trankina frequently visited farmers as far as sixty miles from Cando, ministering in their homes and holding church services. Rae would accompany him to play the portable organ and sing, while the children were expected to provide support. One of the images that stayed with Vince Trankina the rest of his life was his father at a rancher's house reading the Bible by a hurricane lamp, while people drove their horses and sleighs to hear him. They sang hymns while Trankina played the banjo or Autoharp. Payment came to the family in the form of sacks of potatoes, cured hams and other food produced by the farmers. Trankina was always given enough money for gasoline so that he could continue his traveling ministry.

"I feel I have had success spiritually and materially with these people," the Reverend Trankina said, "because I know how they feel."

The Trankinas also ministered to the area's Indian reservations, and extended their evangelical reach beyond Cando to towns such as Drayton, Adams, Devils Lake, Derrick, Edmore, Crocus, Bisbee, Bottineau, Bantry, Lake Metigoshe, Newburg, Turtle Mountains and Maxbass. Trankina also did a live gospel radio broadcast every week on KDLR in Devils Lake. Rae would play the piano, they would sing, and then Joe would deliver a sermon. Again, the children were usually in tow, and it may have been a quartet composed of Trankina and three other locals that first interested young Tony in singing professionally. After each of these broadcasts, one member of the quartet – Curly Haas, a Cando Ford dealer – would take everyone to a restaurant in Devils Lake. For the Trankina children, this was one of the biggest events of the year.

No one, not even Tony Trankina himself, could pinpoint when he first developed his interest in singing. It was, he later recalled, at a very early age, and it was something he didn't have to try very hard to achieve. His voice was clear, high and, with the fluidity of youth, hit the highest of notes with perfect pitch. He began to sing every Sunday in the mission, and while he didn't like interacting with the clientele, he did enjoy singing and used these opportunities to hone his skills.

"Somewhere along the line, I picked up a lot of daydreams," he said. "I wanted to be rich and famous. Perhaps from the movies I occasionally saw or perhaps from reading magazines given us to sell as junk, I got the idea that my world of wealth and fame would be in show business. I thought of little else.

"Whenever I sang at evening services, I wasn't in a mission chapel; I was in a nightclub or a radio studio or cutting a record," he continued. "I memorized Bible verses easily because I looked on the chore as practice for learning lines for a play I'd be in some day. And I never hesitated to tell anybody exactly where I was going in my life, on my own."

Hearing him, his mother would quote from the Book of James, chapter four, verse fourteen: "You know not what you shall be on the morrow. For what is your life? It is just a vapor that appears for a little time and then vanishes away."

Tony knew the verse by heart and understood the warning it conveyed. He rejected it, however, just as he rejected everything about the religion that had made slaves of his parents for drunks and vagrants, and had made his own life bleak and miserable.

By the time he entered his teens, it was obvious to everyone in the Trankina family that his vocal ability was extraordinary. A number of music teachers in the area noticed it, as well, and approached the Trankinas about giving Tony formal lessons. Joe and Rae, however, were reluctant to create bad feelings among

31

any of the teachers, and so they refused all offers. Tony, they decided, would have to remain a natural talent. But there was another reason, as well, grounded in the cold, hard facts of life.

"They all wanted him," said Nina of the music teachers, "but they also wanted to be paid. My parents didn't have the means. They always tried to do what was best for all of us children."

While Tony continued to work and improve on his own – achieving a magnificent, operatic vibrato, stunning lung capacity and admirable control – there was much that only formal lessons could have taught him. Years later, when he was an established singer, he did take singing lessons in Italy. But both his popular and gospel career would be plagued with small but noticeable vocal quirks that critics – particularly during his popular recording career – would be all too happy to point out.

Still, the voice of Tony Trankina was far bigger than anything Cando, North Dakota had ever heard before. As a Cando High School student, he sang in cantatas and received the high school award as tenor soloist for two years. Additionally, he competed in state vocal contests and won a Dakota State Achievement Award. He also was active in sports, occupying a starring position on the high school's basketball team.

His restless desire to break free of the poverty, cold and rural nature of Cando remained constant. Even more than that, now, was his hatred of all things religious. He no longer made a secret of his distaste for God, the mission, and his parents' devotion to serving downtrodden humanity, openly shunning them and arguing their validity with his mother. This hardening atheism troubled Rae Trankina deeply, and she prayed for her rebellious son daily. His reaction was to despise God even more. Once, when his mother said to him, "One day, God is going to use your voice," Tony replied, "I don't want to use it for God. I want to use it for myself."

Tony's progress as a singer attracted the attention of the music department at North Dakota State University, which offered him a musical scholarship upon graduation from high school. Tony, however, had no intention of letting any more time slip away from him. The lights and glitter of the entertainment industry beckoned too strongly. In 1941, in a brazen display of rebellion, the now sixteen-year-old Tony disguised his age by painting a mascara mustache onto his upper lip, and ran away from home with a dance band.

Joe and Rae Trankina weren't about to let their underage son disappear without a trace, at least not yet. They contacted the police, and a statewide alarm was issued. Tony remained on the lam with the band for six weeks, but at last he was spotted, nabbed, and forced to return home. Tony remained recalcitrant and determined to escape his surroundings, and his parents were just as unwavering in their resolution to impose upon him guidelines for acceptable behavior. A compromise was finally reached. Tony could escape his surroundings by moving to Chicago to live with his grandmother on the West End, but he had to continue his high-school education. Tony quickly agreed.

In the city of his father's birth, Tony dutifully attended classes at Austin High School, but at the same time made the rounds of nightclubs trying to break into show business. They all told him to go home. Perhaps it was his youth, or his lack of experience, or both. In response, Tony organized his own band made up of some of his talented high-school friends, and serving as the band's lead singer, began to perform at events throughout Chicago.

The response among Chicagoans was positive, but just as the band began to pick up steam, the world began to change for everyone. The bombing of Pearl Harbor by the Japanese on December 7, 1941, filled young men like Tony Trankina with a sense of outrage and patriotic duty. With the war tocsin sounding, the would-be entertainer remained at his studies as long as he could. Finally, in July of 1943, just before his eighteenth birthday, he went to a Coast Guard recruiting station, lied about his age, and entered the U.S. Armed Forces.

Meanwhile, things were changing back home. Vince had graduated from high school in 1940 and was enrolled at Jamestown College on a football and track scholarship. Joe and Rae Trankina, answering a call to minister in a different part of the country, left Cando in 1942 and moved to Grand Forks,

North Dakota, where they established the Grand Forks Rescue Mission and Service Center.

Even though Tony Trankina would remain in contact with his family, he had left their way of life behind him forever.

Chapter Four

The U.S. Coast Guard played an active and integral role in every major amphibious landing launched by the United States in the Second World War. In 1941, the Coast Guard's ranks boasted only twenty-five thousand officers and enlisted men, but at the height of the war that number surged to two hundred forty-one thousand as the Coast Guard provided convoy escorts, landed troops and armament, maintained coastal and port security, and – taking an even more aggressive role – sank twelve German submarines.

According to records on file with the National Personnel Records Center, Anthony Trankina enlisted in the Coast Guard on July 15, 1943, and the next day was shipped out to the Manhattan Beach Training Station for basic training. His records, which are partially blacked out by the Records Center, indicate his love for singing.

"Hobbies: Is a singer, tenor, ballads, and popular music, also classics and religious music. Has 2 certificated (sic) for State Championship in choir and choral work...(Blacked out section reveals words "Mother," "Father" and "Baptist")...and subject would like to do PHm work. Played drums in swing band."

PHm was, at that time, the Coast Guard abbreviation for a Pharmacist's Mate.

The records also indicate that, in October of 1943, Trankina was at Pier 18, S.T., as part of a boarding detail. His grade is listed as Seaman 2c, and his date and place of discharge were September 7, 1945, in Brooklyn, New York.

After the war, Tony Fontane readily acknowledged his World War II service, but at the same time did not elaborate on it. In interviews, he always gave his Coast Guard service a glancing blow, and what little we know comes from these hit-and-run mentions in newspaper and magazine articles, and from comments he made to friends and family. Based on these sources, we know that he saw combat in the European theater, participated in the Normandy invasion of June 6, 1944, and was wounded. The shrapnel wound in his leg tormented him for the rest of his life, particularly in inclement weather. We also know that at some point he served with a Red Cross entertainment unit overseas. And that is almost all we know, except that he was awarded the American Campaign Medal and the World War II Victory Medal. There is no mention in his records of a Purple Heart, despite the wound he told his daughter, Char, that he had received.

"My father just never talked much about his military service, although he did mention that he'd been wounded," said Char in an interview many years later. "He didn't elaborate on it, though."

One other thing has come down to us from that period. His service in the Coast Guard marked the last time he would ever be known to the world at large as Tony Trankina. After his discharge in 1945, with no intention whatsoever of returning to the bleakness of missionary life in North Dakota, he adopted the stage name of Fontane and set out to get the things he wanted most – money, fame, and a life in the fast lane of show business.

"He plucked the name of Fontane out of thin air," said Char. "No other solo performer was using the name at that time and it was in keeping with his Italian heritage, which was starting to be a popular commodity among singers in the 1940s ."

Indeed. Frank Sinatra was already a household name, and others including Perry Como, Frankie Laine, Johnny Desmond, Vic Damone and Dean Martin would stiffen the competition among singers of Italian heritage. Tony Fontane found himself in New York knocking on the doors of night clubs and record companies to little or no avail. Occasionally a small night club allowed him to perform, but without pay. And Fontane was willing to do it, just to get the experience. But the breaks weren't coming, and around town Fontane quickly became known as a "professional auditioner."

Dirt poor, he lived as cheaply as possible, often sleeping, washing up and changing the few clothes he owned in the men's room of the New York Port Authority before going off to his next audition.

"Knowing my father and his charm, it's entirely possible he

36

found some little old lady somewhere and talked her into doing his laundry for him while he waited," Char said. "I know he had one set of trousers and one shirt, but no jacket. He had a tie, but he had to trade part of his Coast Guard uniform to get it."

Years later, Fontane would tell audiences the story of how he was so broke, and so hungry, that he would go to all-night diners in the wee hours of the morning, sit at the counter and request a small teapot filled with hot water, and a spoon. Condiments, including a bowl filled with soda crackers, were on the counter. Fontane would remove all the crackers from the bowl, pour into it the hot water, and then, from among the condiments, add catsup, salt and pepper, and a few crackers. That bowl of "tomato soup" was, sometimes, his food for the entire day.

If Fontane was discouraged, or even slightly dissuaded, from following his chosen profession, he never showed it and never quit trying. Finally, the persistence and undeniable talent of the young singer paid off. Leaving the unproductive pastures of New York, Fontane made his way back to Chicago where, before World War II, he had achieved some modest successes. It was here that he made one of the most important auditions of his life.

The Major Bowes Amateur Hour was an enormously popular radio show created and hosted by Edward Bowes, who had managed New York's Capitol Theatre in the 1920s. Affected and imperious, Bowes insisted on being addressed as "Major" because the title lent him an air of importance. In 1934, he brought the amateur hour he had created to CBS Radio where, each week, he chatted with contestants and sat in judgment on their performances.

Bowes was famous for his impatience with contestants, particularly when they exhibited little or no talent. Perpetually cross, it seemed, Bowes' brusque, "All right, all right," was a dreaded refrain to young performers vying for the winning slot on his show, and even became a staple for comedians on radio and in the movies. If the performances displeased Bowes, he would either sound a loud bell or strike a gong (a gimmick that gave rise many years later to television's *The Gong Show*). The show went on the road, traveling all over America giving new talent a chance to hit the big time.

By 1945 the Bowes program was not at the height of its popularity, having lost much of its appeal during the war years when audience participation by telephone was limited due to governmental telephone restrictions. But the show was still a success, and had been known to propel young performers to stardom. This was most dramatically evidenced by a very young Frank Sinatra, who not only won the Bowes contest, but also was the only performer to ever be called back for an encore. That is, until Tony Fontane showed up.

Fontane entered one of the road-show versions of the Bowes program and quickly shot to the top of the contender list. His smooth, clear, tenor voice and easy interpretation of popular songs not only captivated the audience, but the moderator, as well. There is no record of what Fontane sang on the program, but it must have been dazzling. He not only won *The Major Bowes Amateur Hour,* but he nudged Sinatra off his pedestal, as well, when he was called him back for an encore.

Riding high, now, Fontane found the doors of night clubs opening for him, and he walked through them confident that the life of fame, fortune, and glamour he had always dreamt of was now within his grasp. The days of frigid and austere North Dakota winters and enforced privation were behind him forever, and he intended to keep it that way.

In February of 1946, following his success on the *Amateur Hour*, Fontane, who was still working and living in Chicago, snagged a regular spot on an ABC radio program, *Teen Town*. Hosted by the buxom blonde beauty Mary Hartline, the show was set in a town run completely by teenagers. Dick York, who would go on to star as Darrin Stephens in the long-running television series, *Bewitched*, portrayed the town's mayor. Hartline served as the show's bandleader and trumpet soloist, while a stream of regulars and special guests provided musical interludes. Tony Fontane was one of these, crooning his way through popular songs and contributing to the program's many skits. His youthful voice and persona quickly netted him a sizeable following among Chicago's teenagers.

But at this point in his career, Fontane's ambitions far exceeded the boundaries of the Windy City. He had his eye on bigger and better things, and toward that end made regular trips back to New York City, where he found himself no longer considered a "professional auditioner." By 1947, success on the Bowes and Hartline programs had put him in the minor celebrity category, which was enough for the Big Apple's nightclub owners. Where once he had been shown the door, or allowed to perform a song without compensation, Fontane was now welcomed into bigger and better nightclubs with open arms, and open checkbooks. The young singer's unique delivery, in which he combined the crooner's art with operatic ability, quickly won over audiences, particularly when he effortlessly hit the highest and longest of notes. Many years later, during his gospel career, Fontane's ability to reach and sustain high notes with perfect control and astonishing power was legendary. "I could read a magazine story while Tony held a note," said one of his accompanists, Burt Lange.

Fontane's ascent on the showbiz ladder continued, mostly through the medium of radio. Although he told an interviewer several years later that his activity in the late 1940s included appearing in several Hollywood short films, there is no official record of these performances. In the same interview Fontane also shaved three years off his real age. It is, however, a matter of record that he created and sold to the Mutual Broadcasting System in Chicago a program in which he served as the star, singing current hits. He also made the rounds of other popular radio shows of the day, including *Top Tunes With Trendler*, a Mutual production featuring orchestra leader Robert Trendler, and Steve Allen's *Smile Time* out of Los Angeles.

Fontane's lifestyle began to reflect his growing popularity, but not in some of the ways common to many performers. He didn't smoke, knowing that it would destroy his voice, and he didn't drink, possibly because of his years of having to deal with drunks in his parents' mission. He was also particular about the women he dated, preferring to pick and choose rather than to widely play the field like some of his contemporaries. His jaunts between Chicago, New York, and Los Angeles put him in touch with some of the kinds of women he liked, including film stars Ann Sheridan and Arlene Dahl, both of whom he briefly dated. Rather, Fontane's growing affluence made it possible for him to indulge his love of fast cars, quality clothes, jewelry, and other material goods. While he hobnobbed with the likes of Frank Sinatra, Dean Martin, and Jerry Lewis in the nightclubs of New York and Chicago, and dated movie stars in Los Angeles, Fontane's life in the fast lane usually involved an imported vehicle.

Despite his successes, Fontane still was mostly a Chicago and New York phenomenon. This would begin to change in 1947-48 when Mercury Records came calling. Founded in Chicago in 1945 by Irving Green, Berle Adams and Arthur Talmadge, Mercury was already making its influence felt in jazz, blues, and country music, and with stars such as Frankie Laine, Vic Damone, and Patti Page, was quickly becoming a force in the popular music market, as well. The addition of Tony Fontane to its stable of singers would increase Mercury's penetration into the pop market, at times dramatically.

Once his career picked up speed and he began to gain renown as a crooner, Fontane returned to his roots in North Dakota to share his gift and his newfound fame with the folks back home. He visited the music class of his former high school, and sang for the school assembly.

"They loved him," recalled Nina. "There was nobody prouder than Joe (Jr.) and I."

Two aspects of Fontane's career at this time remain shrouded in mystery. The first was the spelling of his name. While the singer spelled it "Fontane," Mercury Records routinely spelled it "Fontaine." The variant spelling also found its way into a great deal of printed matter and would continue to do so throughout Fontane's career. Neither he nor anyone else ever explained the discrepancy.

The second mystery is less benign, and lurks even deeper in

the shadows than the misspelling of a name. This centered on the involvement of the Mafia in Tony Fontane's career. While he never spoke of the Mafia in public, he frequently did so with his wife and daughter years after his involvement with the mob had ended. He indicated to them that the Mafia was significantly responsible for his appearances in the night clubs of New York and Chicago, and for his record contract with Mercury. "They owned my contract," he would tell his daughter years later.

"The mob liked my father, and often invited him to join them," Char said. "But Dad very wisely managed to stay his own man, as much as was possible without offending or angering the mobsters who wanted him as a member of the family, so to speak. The real test would come a little ways down the road when he wanted to break his ties with them altogether."

For now, though, Fontane was riding high, even though the songs he recorded for Mercury in the late 1940s – traditional love songs, show tunes and the occasional ballad – weren't chart toppers by any stretch of the imagination. Sales were respectable, teenagers loved him, and Mercury considered him one of their success stories.

But more successes were on the way – big ones – one of which would change his life forever.

Chapter Five

For Tony Fontane, success bred more success. In 1949, his radio performances and recordings with Mercury caught the attention of programmers at WGN, a Chicago television station that had hit the airwaves the previous year. Executives at the station proposed a weekly musical-variety show in which Fontane sang and performed in skits with well-known guests. When Pepsi-Cola stepped up as the sponsor, *The Tony Fontane Show* was born, and aired every Friday at 5:30 p.m. This, plus his weekly appearance on a now-televised *Top Tunes With Trendler* program every Sunday afternoon on WGN, helped enhance Fontane's career profile.

One evening in early 1950, Fontane and his agent found themselves watching a televised interview with two young actresses who had just completed a film with Republic Pictures. The movie was *Prehistoric Women,* and the actresses were Joan Shawlee, who would go on to work as a regular on *The Dick Van Dyke Show* of the 1960s, and Kerry Vaughn, a blonde, curvaceous beauty who had been discovered by Metro Goldwyn Mayer several years earlier. Fontane wasn't particularly interested in the film they had just made, or Shawlee, but he couldn't take his eyes off of Vaughn.

He turned to his agent and said, "That's the woman I'm going to marry."

"Are you nuts?" asked the agent.

"Maybe," said Fontane, turning his eyes once again to the television, "but I'm going to marry her. I want you to contact her and see if she wants to do a guest spot on my show."

The twenty-two-year-old Vaughn agreed to do *The Tony Fontane Show* as a way to help promote *Prehistoric Women,* which ultimately wouldn't be released in the United States until November of that year. When she finally appeared on the program in February of 1950, she found that her host was completely smitten with her. But Vaughn, whose classic features and voluptuous figure were rivaled only by her cool, self-assured elegance, was anything but smitten with Fontane. To her, he seemed like just another hot-blooded entertainment type bent on wooing her – a type with which she'd had lots of experience in her short Hollywood career. Already she had dated some of the industry's most famous leading men, including notorious lady-killer Errol Flynn, and when she met Fontane she was seeing, simultaneously, Gene Kelly, Robert Stack and Victor Mature. She appreciated Fontane's singing, but was less than excited about the teen idol's advances.

Vaughn was born on January 29, 1927, in Miami, Florida. Her architect father, Cylon Vaughn, and his wife, Charlotte, moved to Houston, Texas, shortly after their daughter's birth, and it was here that Vaughn grew into a skinny, gangly youngster with thin limbs, awkward bearing, and a wild shock of thick blonde hair. She considered herself an ugly duckling, and every night for two years prayed that God would let her wake up the next morning looking like Lana Turner. And it very nearly happened that way. Between the ages of twelve and thirteen, Vaughn's face and figure blossomed to the point where even her classmates hardly recognized her. By the time she was fourteen, Vaughn was arrestingly beautiful, and mature far beyond her years.

In the summer of 1941, Vaughn and a girlfriend were lunching in a small Houston diner when a man walked up to their booth and told them he was a Metro Goldwyn Mayer movie scout working for producer Walter Wanger. He said he was seeking the "ten most beautiful women in the world" to work for MGM, and that Vaughn was on his short list.

"Even at that age my mother was pretty savvy," said Char in 2004, "so she said to him, 'Yeah, yeah, give me your card, if you're serious – but you'll have to talk to my dad.'"

To Vaughn's surprise, the scout was authentic, and made an appointment to meet her father that night. At the Vaughn home, he laid out his case for Kerry to travel to Hollywood – her parents in tow, of course – for a career as an actress, with general education classes to be provided by the studio. The offer seemed too good to pass up, so within a month Vaughn and her mother took a train to Los Angeles where the fourteen-year-old signed an MGM contract. Her father transplanted his architecture business from Houston to Los Angeles, and the family lived in a Swiss chalet-style cottage on Glen Green Terrace in Hollywood Hills.

Although the official record doesn't credit Vaughn for movie work until 1944, she reportedly filled uncredited bit parts in a number of films of the early 1940s, including several in the Andy Hardy series. Most of her time, though, was spent in training, and she received the best voice, dancing, and acting lessons the studio could provide, attending drama school with Debbie Reynolds and Janet Leigh. Vaughn became an accomplished dancer and singer, and by 1944 was entertaining the troops at the Hollywood Canteen along with her much more famous contemporaries.

Also in 1944, Vaughn snagged bit parts in *Atlantic City* and *Dancing in Manhattan*, both B-level films, and received no credit for either appearance. While 1945 was busier for her, Vaughn still couldn't seem to get her name on a movie screen. She had an uncredited part as a guest at Mayfair tea in *The Picture of Dorian Gray*, and received no credit as a bathing beauty in the Pat O'Brien film, H*aving Wonderful Crime*. She was likewise unbilled as a "Salome girl" in the Yvonne De Carlo film *Salome Where She Danced*, a chorus girl in Merle Oberon's *This Love of Ours*, a hostess in *Frontier Gal* (again with De Carlo), and as a "blonde girl" in the Edward G. Robinson classic, *Scarlet Street*.

Despite her beauty and talent, Kerry Vaughn was just one of thousands of gifted, gorgeous young women in Hollywood in the 1940s, and her career as an actress never took off. She herself was, in large part, to blame. Many years later she confided to her daughter that she never really had the desire to succeed in films, mostly because she was fearful that she wasn't a good enough actress. "My looks," she said, "were really all I had." Vaughn's failure to crystallize with the studio star makers, or the public at large, resulted in her being loaned out to other studios as early as 1944, including Republic, Columbia, RKO, Universal, and Fritz Lang Productions. Even when it seemed that Fate might intervene – in the late 1940s, Vaughn was once used in long shots to fill in for a drunk and absent Lana Turner – she continued to perform under the radar screen, never really getting the break that would propel her to stardom. *Prehistoric Women* wasn't going to change anything, at least not in Vaughn's immediate career.

The so-called story line of the movie, which was shot at the Ray Corrigan Ranch in Simi Valley, California, and at Hollywood's General Service Studio, is sophomoric. A clan of man-hating cave women, realizing they need men in order to perpetuate the species, take a few men prisoner as potential husbands. One of these men, Engor, discovers fire, fights a monster that strongly resembles a big rubber chicken, and wins the hand of the queen of the man-hating clan. Starring Laurette Luez, Allan Nixon, Joan Shawlee, Judy Landon, Mara Lynn, and Vaughn as Tulee, one of the fur-clad prehistoric babes, *Prehistoric Women* was B movie material from start to finish. Yet, when it was released on the exploitation circuit with the tagline "Savage! Primitive! Deadly!," it allegedly made a ton of money for producer Albert J. Cohen. Today, the film is considered a cult classic, if not a particularly good film.

After appearing on Fontane's television show in February of 1950, Vaughn found herself relentlessly pursued by the singer. In the film they would make together twelve years later, *The Tony Fontane Story*, their courtship is depicted as one of cool reluctance on her part and eager-beaver fervor on his, and the dramatization hits fairly close to the mark. But even Vaughn's self possession and haughty reserve crumbled under Fontane's relentless attentions and boyish charm. After three whirlwind months, during which Fontane even followed Vaughn around the country on promotional tours for *Prehistoric Women* just to be near her, Vaughn succumbed and agreed to marry him.

"My mother said there were two things that got her to marry my father," said Char. "The first thing was his talent, and the second thing was his sweetness and innocence, that he had an innocence about him that, no matter how wild he tried to be, he had this pureness of spirit that she had never come across.

"Now, she had dated Clark Gable, Errol Flynn, everybody, and she said she had come across a few gentlemen, such as William Powell. But she told me she never met anyone who had the heart of my father, and she fell in love with that and with his amazing voice."

The prophesy Fontane had made to his agent came true on May 2, 1950. Fontane and Kerry Vaughn were married at Chicago City Hall by District Judge Rudolph Desort during a break in a murder trial. Their honeymoon lasted one day at the Drake Hotel in Chicago. The next day it was back to work, with Fontane continuing to perform on television and to record for Mercury. While Vaughn's film career was coming to a close with the release of *Prehistoric Women* – she would appear in only one other commercially produced movie, as a cocktail waitress in 1952's *Something To Live For*, directed by George Stevens – her talent as a singer and dancer made her a perfect choice for nightclubs and other stage acts.

Fontane was, at this time, primarily a teen idol, crooning out love songs calculated to pluck the heartstrings of the young and emotional. Often referred to in print as Tony "Fontaine", he received a number of good notices, including the cover story in the April 14, 1951, edition of *TV Forecast*. While the story failed to mention his recent marriage and inaccurately stated Fontane's age as twenty-three – he was almost twenty-six – it still managed to capture the essence of the singer and his appeal to a young audience:

> When Tony Fontaine (sic) sings, teenage girls undergo some sort of physical evolution. Heartbeats slow down. Eyelids flutter softly. Moist little hands twist nervously at handkerchiefs. Faces grow taut with torment.
>
> The young man who inspires this type of mystic torture probably doesn't give it much thought, and would rather let the psychologists figure it out. Next to singing, Tony Fontaine would rather be munching banana splits.
>
> He's a handsome young tenor of 23 years of age who has stockpiled a pleasing combination of voice and manners into a brace of WGN-TV shows – *Top Tunes With Trendler* and *The Tony Fontaine Show*.

More than that, Tony is a Chicagoland boy who came back home to make good. With the solid backing of the local teen set, the Fontaine star has started to climb in the entertainment heavens.

Besides his TV stints, Tony has done well in the radio and the record field. Some of his disks that move briskly are "Stranger In the City," "To Love You Is Madness" and his latest, "Vision of Bernadette." His hobbies are painting and collecting ties.

After giving his early life a glossy once-over that completely omitted his one-time poverty and current atheism, *TV Forecast* continued with a glowing account of Fontane's growing fame:

Deep in the juke box bistros where earnest young talent gather, is whispered in hushed tones the legend of the Bowes encore. In all history, only two performers were ever called back for one. The first was Frank Sinatra, the second was Tony Fontaine.

Not content with this fling at immortality, Tony junketed among theater appearances, teen radio shows and Hollywood movie shorts. The prodigal son finally returned to Chicago where he is now getting the right kind of breaks in show business.

On the human interest side, there's a young lady in Tony's life named Carol. He is very fond of her. Carol hasn't walked or talked since she was three years old, but she heard Tony one night and asked her mother to write for his picture.

Tony delivered it in person and fell in love with Carol. Now he visits her regularly, in fact, has helped her in learning to talk. Carol is just 12 years old.

The rise of Fontaine has helped to keynote a phenomenon peculiar to U.S. vocalizing – the widespread monopoly enjoyed by crooners of Italian descent…Irish Bing Crosby, of course, splits the field, but technically he's a singer of ballads, not a crooner.

And yet, while Fontane possessed a voice of rare power and beauty, his lack of formal musical training routinely demonstrated itself in his recordings. Sometimes his tremulous, high-vibrato delivery on every word of a song struck reviewers as a bit much, and sometimes a lack of control made his singing seem, to them, overly emotional.

Mercury's release of "A Friend of Johnny's" and "To Love You Is Madness," prompted a reviewer for the March 9, 1951, edition of *Downbeat Magazine* to write:

"Tony is the lad who has found sudden popularity in Chicago via two or three regular TV and radio shows. But he shows little on these tunes, getting an unnecessary tear-jerking quality and using a too-pronounced attack, then vibrato, on many words. There (is) no feeling of relaxation."

However, the reviewer did note that "The piano solo on 'Johnny's' is surprisingly modern."

And four months later, a different reviewer for the same magazine wrote in the July 27, 1951, edition about Mercury's release of "Jug of Wine" and "Losing You:"

"Tony does pretty well on 'Losing,' though his control has a rough time, in spots, and the rhythm section in the George Bassman-conducted orchestra sounds unrelaxed. On 'Jug,' Fontaine whines on 'wine' and his voice has none of the necessary quality another young singer, one Bill Farrell, once unwittingly boasted about."

The critics at *Downbeat* weren't unloading on Fontane because they disliked him or because they fitted one wag's description of a music critic – "a man whose wife ran off with a singer." Rather, the observers for *Downbeat* made valid points which, had he heeded them, might have helped Fontane with a genre of music that didn't really allow his voice its full potential. His lack of formal training and unusual accenting of certain words made him seem, at times, uncomfortable or restive within the songs, and there's little doubt that structured musical training would have given Fontane the vocal discipline and interpretive fine-tuning the critics felt he needed.

Despite Fontane's less-than-operatic perfection and the observations of some of the critics, teens adored this boyishly handsome young singer with the strong, clear voice, and put their money where their affections lay. In June of 1951, at the same time critics for *Downbeat Magazine* were pointing out Fontane's singing flaws, two of his songs – "The Syncopated Clock" and "Bring Back the Thrill" – were on the list of twenty-five top tunes for songs played on the radio, and for record and sheet music sales. Granted, neither song provided much of a venue for Fontane's talents, especially the Leroy Anderson ditty "The Syncopated Clock," which gave Fontane little opportunity to do anything other than prove he could carry a tune. And yet, the song charted at number twelve in 1951, bringing Fontane yet another measure of success. Two months later, in August of 1951, the song remained on the list and had been joined by Fontane's rendition of "Vanity," the Bernie Bierman composition that also found expression that year with Sarah Vaughn, Don Cherry, Hadda Brooks, saxophonist Don Byas and bandleader Enoch Light.

Shortly after the release of "The Syncopated Clock," Fontane realized a longtime dream when Ed Sullivan invited him to appear on his nationally broadcast weekly television show, *Toast of the Town,* which was the predecessor to *The Ed Sullivan Show*. On July 29, 1951, Fontane sang live in a show replete with talent of the day, including Yul Brynner, Cab Calloway, Rose Marie, and Pinky Lee.

Life, at least in terms of his career, was a mixed blessing for Fontane. Although he was busier than ever, he had yet to achieve a true hit recording, one that set him apart from the many talented nightclub, radio, and recording artists plying their trade in the U.S. at that time. Despite his successes, he still remained essentially a mid-level performer whose national fame was far below the likes of Frank Sinatra, Dean Martin or Frankie Laine.

In 1951, however, a song written by country music star Hank Williams went through the roof of the popular charts when it was sung by crooner Tony Bennett. "Cold, Cold Heart" was an instant success, and someone at Mercury Records suggested that Tony Fontane sing a version. Fontane, whose heart, soul and voice were more attuned to the music and style of Mario Lanza than Hank Williams, flatly refused. Many years later, one of his accompanists on the gospel-music tour, Burt Lange, said Fontane agreed to sing the song, but "someone had to slip him five hundred bucks to do it." In any event, Fontane recorded "Cold, Cold Heart," saw it released in November of 1951, and then watched it rocket up the popular-music charts. It peaked at number eight, sold 1.3 million disks, and earned Fontane the one thing his career needed most – a Gold Record. Its success played a major role in *Billboard* magazine ranking Fontane sixth most popular male vocalist of 1951.

"Cold, Cold Heart" triggered a series of professional opportunities for Fontane. In quick succession he appeared on the television shows of Steve Allen, Paul Whiteman, Hoagy Carmichael, Eddie Bracken and Robert Q. Lewis. Ed Sullivan invited him back. On the turntables of America, Fontane could now be found sharing space with the likes of Patti Page, Sophie Tucker and Tony Martin on the popular *Showboat* album, and Frankie Lane, Vic Damone, and Billy Daniels on the Mercury pressing, *On the Sunny Side of the Street*. His own television offering, *The Tony Fontane Show*, was now broadcast from Los Angeles coast-to-coast, and a spin-off of its songs-and-skits format was recreated for radio. The Fontanes had by now moved from Chicago to 2556 Glen Green Terrace in Hollywood Hills.

Occasionally Fontane would travel to see his parents in Grand Forks, but his hatred for God, the mission, and everything they represented in his life had not abated. Whenever he visited, he couldn't wait to get out again, and return to the life of glamour he had worked so hard to attain. Not even when his mother developed spinal cancer, and begged him to pray with her, would Fontane relent. In a March 1968 edition of *Guideposts*, Fontane wrote of his hardness of heart:

Leaving this exciting world even briefly, and even for a reason as serious as my mother's life, bitterly depressed me. The sight of my mother, withering away from cancer of the spine, aroused all my old resentments. I asked her, "Is this the way God treats people who love Him?"

"Don't say that, Tony," she said. "Pray with me. I want to be able to accept God's will."

"Let's pray for a miracle," I suggested, taunting her. "You've got one coming. You've worked hard enough for it."

"The only miracle I want," she said, "is to have enough love for God that I can accept His will for me now. Pray with me, son."

"No," I said, "I don't pray any more. I don't think I've ever really prayed in my life."

By late 1951, Kerry was very pregnant, and exhibiting many of the curious cravings common to expectant women.

"There were two things I would ask of your father," Kerry told Char many years later. "Every single night between two and four in the morning, he would have to go get me Chinese almond cookies. Then I'd want him to sing songs from *Pagliacci*. And every night, he'd do it."

On January 12, 1952, a baby girl was born to Kerry and Tony Fontane at Temple Hospital in Los Angeles. The 5:05 p.m. arrival was named Kerry Char'ae Fontane – Kerry after her mother, and Char'ae as a contraction of Charlotte (Kerry's mother) and Rae (Tony's mother). The baby weighed seven pounds, four ounces, and was described by Kerry in a silk-bound baby book as, simply, "Beautiful!" An additional note observed that "Baby resembles Daddy with Mother's nose. Daddy's temper!"

Raphaela Trankina, whose spinal cancer had bedridden her for the final months of her life, died on March 28, 1952, at the age of forty-eight. Fontane, who returned to Grand Forks for the funeral and sang "Tell Mother I'll Be There," couldn't shake a deep and abiding sense of guilt for having spurned his mother's pleas for prayer. Perhaps it was this guilt that led him to develop a premonition that he, too, would die at the age of forty-eight. At any rate, he wasted no time in putting Grand Forks behind him once again.

"As soon as I could after Mother's death," he wrote years later, "I was on my way out of Grand Forks, again feeling free and relieved."

Chapter Six

Like many entertainers, Fontane sometimes displayed a fondness for sabotaging his own career. Had he gotten his way, he would never have recorded "Cold, Cold Heart." Later, in his gospel-singing days, he routinely turned down offers from professional managers to handle his bookings and recordings, and, as a result, sometimes found himself short of cash and producing records not up to industry standards. It was with the same sense of surety that he decided, in 1953, to manage his own bookings. Not only were nightclubs around the world now clamoring for the young singer to grace their stages – as had the Hollywood Palladium, the Boulevard Room in New York, the Chez Paree in Chicago, the Olympic Theatre in Miami, and the Copa in Pittsburgh – but an Australian reprise of a successful London show also held out an offer that would include both Fontane and Kerry in the cast. In cooperation with David N. Martin and the Tivoli Theatre, Fontane decided to abandon the momentum he had generated in the United States, manage his own bookings, and accept a role in Emile Littler's musical, *Zip Goes A Million*, based on the novel, *Brewster's Millions*. He packed up his wife and baby daughter, boarded the R.M.S. *Oronsay* on March 15, 1953, and headed Down Under to tour with the show.

Zip Goes A Million seemingly had everything going for it. The show had run in London for two years to overflow crowds, and when it traveled to Australia, Emile Littler traveled with it. Littler, who was the director of sixteen London West End theaters and a half owner of three others, became the first British theater manager to actually sail to Australia to supervise the production of his own show. With a cast that included comic actor Roy Barbour, American dancer Margaret Brown and actress Nina Cooke, *Zip* was expected by its producers and cast to be a big hit with Australians, as it had been with the Brits.

Fontane, playing the part of Buddy Delaney, received third billing, and sang the songs "The Thing About You," "It Takes No Time To Fall In Love," "Nothing Breaks But the Heart," and

"Running Away To Land," and joined the rest of the company in a number of other songs. The show's program featured a photo of a smiling, dark-haired Fontane, and a mini-biography that touched on the singer's up-and-down ride in the entertainment industry:

> Tony Fontane, young American recording, TV and stage star, owes his success as a singer to three things: hard work, the ability to sing songs of all types, from jazz to opera, and something with which no one can do without – luck.
>
> Of course, the encouragement given by his beautiful wife Kerry Vaughn (also in *Zip Goes A Million*) helped in no small way.
>
> From the time of his first professional engagement, on a National Teenage radio programme, Tony has struggled, not always successfully, through every branch and class of show business. This early struggle accounts for his ability now to be able to sing all kinds of songs to all kinds of audiences and gain maximum approval...

After detailing Fontane's career credentials, the program noted that "it is indeed seldom that Australian audiences have received the opportunity to enjoy the talents of any singer as outstanding as Tony Fontane..."

In the biography for Kerry, who played the part of Paula Van Norden, the program noted that "Just before leaving America, MGM offered Kerry a starring role in a Technicolor musical opposite Jane Powell, which she refused because of her commitment to come to Australia with her husband, Tony Fontane." If true, the film in question was probably *Small Town Girl*, which was produced by MGM in 1953, and featured Jane Powell, Farley Granger and Ann Miller.

Zip Goes A Million began its Australian tour in Melbourne, then traveled to Sydney and other points throughout the country. Char recalled sleeping in the drawer of her parents' steamer trunk as they traveled with the show, and for the rest of her life, remembered the inside lining of that trunk. She also recounted in a 2005 interview a humorous incident involving her handsome father, a flirtatious showgirl, and an angry wife.

"Women would go around in their showgirl outfits, pasties stuck on, very scantily dressed," Char said. "One night, my mother was coming down the back stairs of the theater. Just at that moment, this very large-busted, pasty-adorned showgirl purposely dropped something in front of my father.

"Dad, ever the gentleman, bent down to pick it up – and so did the showgirl, at exactly the same time. Needless to say, he got an eyeful. He was really embarrassed by that kind of stuff, and turned beet red. The showgirl looked up at Mom, raised her eyebrow, and started laughing.

"Mom at the time was spritzing herself with an atomizer, and got so mad she hauled off and threw the thing at the showgirl. Only she missed, and hit my father in the head, instead, which was okay with her, because she was mad at him, too. My father, who had a bad temper, got furious with her, asking – at the top of his lungs – if she really thought there had been any hanky-panky going on.

"My Mom replied, 'That's irrelevant. You should have just walked away.' They didn't speak to each other for two days after that."

Normally, said Char, her mother exhibited her temper in quieter ways, while her father's style was to "rant and rave."

"I once asked my mother what she would have done if my father had ever stepped out on her," Char said. "I asked, would you try to kill him? She said, 'Well....not right away. I wouldn't mention it, but a year and a half later there'd be poison in the soup.'"

Fontane, however, remained hopelessly in love with his wife, and entertained no notions of stepping out on her. He was a charmer, with a big, beautiful smile and a relaxed, friendly manner. Kerry knew that, accepted it, and admitted to Char that Fontane, while having lived the glittering life of a Hollywood entertainer, was no gadabout. "He had this thing about purity in his body," Kerry said. "But he gave the impression of being just the opposite. He was full of life and vibrancy, and women came on to him. He was a very passionate man, but only with me."

But when it came to other men flirting with his wife, Fontane was known to let his explosive temper get the best of him. Once, when out driving with Kerry and Char, a man in another car leered over at the Fontane vehicle and made an off-color remark about Kerry. Fontane lost control. He used his car to cut off and bring to a stop the other motorist. As Fontane leaped out of his car, the motorist quickly rolled up his window. Undaunted, Fontane punched out the driver's window and, with a bloodied fist, grabbed the now terrified motorist by his neck.

"This is my wife," growled Fontane. "Respect her, or you'll have no face." Cowed the motorist apologized profusely for his behavior.

It was during the family's time in Australia that Char made her entertainment debut. On August 6, 1953, at the age of nineteen months, she appeared as a model in the J.W. Robinson Company Christmas catalog. Several months later Char made a much more conspicuous, if not auspicious, debut when she slipped away from a nanny and wandered, completely naked, onto the stage where her mother and father were performing. *The Sydney Daily Mirror* noted that "it brought the house down."

Despite its provenance, *Zip Goes A Million* was a flop in Australia. Frank Doherty, writing in the November 1, 1954, *Melbourne Argus*, noted in his headline that "*Zip* Is Short of Zip." The few positive comments he made in his review were about Tony and Kerry, and he was the first of many entertainment writers to note the physical similarities between Kerry and Marilyn Monroe.

> With the help of some better-than-average lyrics and one or two presentable tunes this musical version of the old *Brewster's Millions* farce lifts itself a little above the ordinary.
>
> The story is trite and harmless, but a little ingenuity would come in handy.

Jokes about the nationalisation of Britain's railway system, even if they do give an opportunity for Roy Barbour to bring in the chestnut-group story about two trains colliding in the "biggest dam' crash you ever saw," have little point in this country, and certainly no topicality.

Mr. Barbour is a comedian in the George Formby tradition, with flaat voice, flaat caap and flaat feet. He works hard for his laughs but they are few and scattered miserly through two acts.

Miss Nina Cooke sings charmingly but should never have been cast as a winsome Lancashire girl. The part is unworthy of her. Margaret Brown and Kerry Vaughn are much happier with their roles which give them little to do except (for the first) dance and sing a little and (for the second) continue to look like Marilyn Monroe.

Tony Fontane in the juvenile lead did, at least, understand the meaning of the word "zip" and put it into his work. His voice is both strong and pleasant.

In 1955, shortly after the cast of *Zip Goes A Million* threw a birthday party for three-year-old Char at the Tivoli Theatre in Sydney, the show closed. Fontane, however, was quickly given a role in another Tivoli Theatre musical making the rounds in Australia, *Paint Your Wagon*. His performance in a role that, years later, would be played in the movies by Clint Eastwood, would prove to be much more of a career booster than had the ill-fated *Zip*. In Sydney, Fontane recorded a number of songs featured in *Paint Your Wagon*, and one of them – Lerner and Loewe's "I Talk To The Trees" – soared to the top of the Australian pop charts. The song remained at the number one position on the Australian Hit Parade for sixteen consecutive weeks, and made a star out of Tony Fontane half a world away from the United States. At about this time he also recorded an album for Columbia Records, *Songs By the Fireside*, which paired Fontane with one of the country's most popular orchestras, Bob Gibson and his Velvet Strings. With trumpeter Alan Nash on hand, the eight-cut album featured Fontane at his smoothest and best, warbling songs about fire ("I Don't Want To Set the World On Fire"), smoke ("Smoke Gets In Your Eyes") and passion ("My Old Flame").

Before he left *Paint Your Wagon* in 1955 to perform in a series of nightclubs around the world, he made a farewell radio appearance on the nationally popular *The Ford Show*, singing "Try A Little Tenderness" ("Because my wife likes it," he told the audience), and a bold, energetic version of "I'm Gonna Live Till I Die." Then, with wife and daughter in tow, Fontane embarked on a whirlwind tour, performing in New Zealand, Singapore, Toronto, Paris, and, finally, London. It was here that Fontane, as a part of one of the famed "Command Performances," sang for Queen Elizabeth II, with Kerry serving as mistress of ceremonies for the event. It was also at the performance that Fontane met one of Kerry's old flames – Errol Flynn. According to Char, Fontane and the aging movie swashbuckler hit it off, and even "hung out" together for awhile. But the chasm between their lifestyles was too great for a very long or lasting friendship.

"Flynn was a big, big drinker, and a serious womanizer, and Dad was neither of those," Char said. "Which is interesting. With all his craziness and wildness, he never smoked, never drank, and he never did drugs. It wasn't a religious thing, especially at that point in his life, just a personal preference. He had this thing about cleanliness, used to wash his hands all the time. He just wanted to keep his body clean, inside and out. That definitely wasn't one of Errol Flynn's big concerns."

The Fontanes returned to the United States on August 4, 1955, and set up housekeeping at 7426 Kelvin Avenue in Canoga Park, California. Fontane, whose successes in Australia had seen a corresponding lapse of popularity in the United States, quickly moved to re-establish himself at home. Again, his involvement with the Mafia is perhaps the murkiest part of his life, but since organized crime controlled many big-city nightclubs and had had a hand in Fontane's first contract with Mercury, it is very likely that the Mob helped get him back into the recording studio and onto the stages of nightclubs. The thirty-year-old singer now signed with Capitol Records, and became a regular act in Las Vegas, pulling in as much as $10,000 a week for his performances there, and in nightclubs in Los Angeles, Chicago, and New York, as well. His daughter remembers visits to the house by mobsters, one of whom she said was an uncle.

"My father often talked of the dichotomy in the lives of those men," she said. "He said they went to church every Sunday, were very kind to people within their families. But they would cut somebody up in an instant, and say, 'God wanted me to do it.'"

It was about this time that the Mafia, for the second time, came to Fontane and told him they wanted him to become a family member. As had been the case when he was a younger man, just starting out in the entertainment industry, Fontane declined, knowing full well that to reject the Mob could translate into a death sentence at worst or, at best, an inability to work in nightclubs. Not long after his refusal, a box arrived at the Fontane residence. Fontane sent Kerry and Char into a bedroom, then carefully opened the box. It contained flowers, and a note that said, "Go in peace."

"That was one of the emotionally defining moments in his life, I can tell you," said Burt Lange years later. "You just don't submit a letter of resignation to the Mafia."

Although Fontane finally relinquished the task of handling his own bookings to professionals – he was represented, now, by the William Morris agency – he did make one foray into independent record producing. In conjunction with Glenwood Music Corporation, he cut a 45 r.p.m. record on the Kerry label (named after his wife), which featured Fontane singing "I'm Your Boy" and, on the flip side, "Dream Dust." The target audience was the teenager of 1956 and the style of the songs can only be described as a cross between edgy jazz and embryonic rock and roll. Fontane didn't even sound like himself in the songs, and the recordings went nowhere.

Kerry, meanwhile, had completely turned her back on her acting career, and was now focused on raising Char'ae. She doted on the girl, and kept meticulous notes about her development. The child's favorite games, Kerry noted, were "dolls, and driving her mother crazy!" Her favorite pastimes were listed as "singing and thinking." And, after a birthday party attended by fourteen neighborhood children, Kerry wrote that "Char'ae was the most beautiful little girl of all. She looked lovely and sang a song beautifully at the party." Char had a dog named Sand and a cat named Syme, appeared on a Los Angeles children's television show in 1956, and lived a life of love and privilege. And Fontane, despite his atheism and detestation of all things religious, allowed Kerry to enroll Char in a Sunday School class, which she did in August of 1956 at the First Baptist Church of Canoga Park.

One year later, Fontane was moving back on track professionally, and his personal life gave him a source of great joy, as well.

"I was living like a king," he wrote for *Guideposts*. "I had my own TV show. I had a beautiful wife, a beautiful daughter, a beautiful home, foreign cars – my self-made world in my hands."

And then, on September 3, 1957, at the intersection of Balboa Boulevard and Sherman Way, the dream world that Tony Fontane had created for himself ended in a nightmare of twisted metal, blood, and unfathomable pain. Another world would slowly but inexorably take the place of that dream existence, one that would give Tony Fontane the rare opportunity to affect not only his own life, but the lives of untold millions, as well.

All he had to do was to keep his side of a bargain with God.

Chapter Seven

When Kerry brought Fontane home from the hospital in late 1957, the singer was, figuratively, a shadow of his former robust self. His injuries, although no longer life threatening, riddled his body with excruciating pain. He had lost weight, and migraine headaches blinded him. "When he got those headaches," his daughter reminisced, "you couldn't even breathe in the house." He couldn't walk, and was confined to a wheelchair. Gradually he struggled out of the wheelchair and onto a pair of crutches.

Most disturbing of all, though, was that Fontane had utterly lost his ability to sing. The crushing of his chest and the damage to his head had robbed him of the once powerful, clear singing voice that represented not only his ability to make a living, but his means of self-identification, as well. His attempts to sing brought only pain, and a croak, from a throat that had once filled nightclubs, theaters and recording studios with strength and lyric beauty. He could only speak in a whisper, and his doctors weren't optimistic. They told him he might be able to sing again, but that he shouldn't try for four to five years, just to give himself time to heal and to avoid further injury.

Later, Fontane said in an interview with *The King's Business,* a magazine produced by Biola University, that he "didn't worry or even think about it," that his newfound faith had given him "such peace." But that's not the way his daughter remembered it, nor is it the way the situation was presented in *The Tony Fontane Story* in 1962, or in a feature story for *Sacred Sound* magazine in 1961. Those sources paint a portrait of a man plunged into the depths of despair.

"I don't understand why I have my life back, if I don't have my voice," Char recalled him as saying, often near the point of tears. "I don't understand what I'm supposed to do."

At one point, he even said, "If there is a God, then show me, pal!"

Kerry was unfailingly supportive, and always tried to console him that his singing voice would, indeed, come back. But it didn't, and as time passed, Fontane became increasingly depressed. His new faith sorely tested, now, he once cried out to God in a tortured whisper, "I want to use this gift for you. Why aren't you letting me?"

And then the thought came to him that would, forever, change his life. After weeks of anguish, despair, explosive displays of temper, impatience, agony, and doubt, Fontane quietly knelt in prayer and made what would become one of the most famous deals with God in the annals of modern Christian history.

"If you give me my voice back," he said, "I promise I will sing only for you."

In *The Tony Fontane Story*, produced by Gospel Films, Fontane, playing himself, is depicted as offering up the prayer and then suddenly bursting into full song, his prayer immediately answered. That moment, like some others in the film, was overly dramatized for effect, and was unreflective of what really happened. In reality, Fontane offered up his prayer, and then began a long, torturous road of vocal rehabilitation, struggling each day to eke out a note here, a note there. He would listen to the radio and silently sing along, straining to make a sound until, one day, the recalcitrant vocal chords responded, and the familiar tenor voice of Tony Fontane began to emerge like a new morning.

Heartened, Fontane pushed himself, and discovered as he practiced that his voice had undergone a change. Where once it had been merely powerful, now it burst forth with a previously untapped energy and vibrancy. Always one to effortlessly hit the high notes and to hold them for incredibly long periods, Fontane now became able to reach even higher, with greater ease, and more flexibility. The timbre of his voice became richer, warmer, and more layered. God, he now knew, had not only restored his voice, but had given him an instrument of greater authority than the one he had previously possessed. Within just a few years, Ethel Waters, the Oscar nominated blues and gospel vocalist, would describe Tony Fontane as "The man with God in his voice."

As his voice returned to him, Fontane realized he had to do two things: keep his side of the bargain with God, and somehow make a living. Achieving those goals, he knew, would pose something of a problem. He was still under contract to the William Morris Agency, which was eager to get their singer back into nightclubs and television and recording studios. How was he going to turn his back on all that, and yet earn an income? More to the point, how would William Morris respond to a singer who refused to accept nightclub singing engagements, or to participate in anything not associated with the glorification of God?

The agency didn't respond graciously. It viewed with a cold eye Fontane's faith and his dedication to it, and looked with an even frostier eye upon his refusal to return to performing popular music. Char recalls that her father "didn't try very hard to convince them," being absolutely sure that what he was doing was the right thing. As a last-ditch effort, William Morris offered him a plum Las Vegas singing engagement, and even sent an agent to Fontane's house to convince him to accept it. Fontane was immoveable.

"This is it," he told the agent. "This is what I'm doing now, and I have no compromises to make with you. I won't do it."

The agency sued for breach of contract. Fontane didn't have a leg to stand on, and the court sided with William Morris. All the money that Fontane had accumulated over the years was, in an instant, wiped out when the agency won its lawsuit. For the second time in his life, Fontane was living in poverty. With a wife, a child, and a home to keep, an unemployed Fontane found himself in dire straits.

"We went from living very, very well to being very, very poor," said Char.

Even though he was still recovering from his injuries, Fontane took work mowing lawns, cleaning gutters, pumping gas, running errands, and helping on construction sites. The man who had once thrilled audiences around the world with his clarion, tenor voice even waited tables, just to bring in some much-needed cash.

"He took it on the chin," Char noted. "I don't ever recall him complaining. I do remember going to bed and hearing discussions in the living room between my parents, and Dad saying to Mom, 'I'm sorry, Kerry, that I've been such a disappointment to you.' And she would always say, 'It'll be fine. You're not a disappointment.'"

But Fontane wasn't just hoping and waiting for an opportunity to sing God's praises. As his voice returned to him, he began writing letters to churches asking them to let him sing. Incredibly, they weren't interested. Fontane's reputation as a nightclub entertainer who hobnobbed with mobsters and lived a glitzy, Godless life, was well known, and the churches he contacted either politely refused him, or simply didn't respond.

"They didn't trust him," recalled Char, "and I remember Dad saying, 'They don't have a reason to trust me, they don't believe this is real.' He was very discouraged, because his conversion was real. Mom, of course, stood by him, and propped him up."

When things looked bleakest, he made a call to an agent friend, who told him he could book Fontane into a Las Vegas nightclub right away. Fontane would make more in six weeks than he'd earned in the last year. Broke, with his very home now in jeopardy, Fontane struggled with the decision he had to make.

Just as he was on the verge of picking up the telephone to accept the nightclub offer, six-year-old Char asked him if anyone could come to Las Vegas to hear him sing. Fontane replied that yes, any adult could come into the nightclub to hear him. After a pause, Char said, "What would you do if Jesus walked in?" And that was it. Fontane, smiling, said, "Yes, what would I do if Jesus walked in?" He never made the telephone call.

That door was closed, forever, but another was about to open – one that would never, ever shut, while Fontane lived. In September of 1958, a man unknown to Fontane, the Reverend Phil Kerr, wrote him a letter. Kerr, a talented Christian singer, songwriter and pianist, had organized the Phil Kerr Monday Night Musicals in 1945 as a way to present to the public top-notch Christian entertainment. In 1958, the musicals were held in the Pasadena Civic Auditorium, and it was here that Kerr asked Tony Fontane to perform. Fontane jumped at the chance.

He first met Kerr and several organizers of the Monday

Night Musicals at a banquet at the Foursquare Church in Burbank, California. Dean Brown, who often led the singing at the Monday night galas, recalled that first meeting:

"Phil said to me, 'There is a young singer who recently became a Christian, and I've asked him to come and meet us tonight. Would you please go outside and see if he has arrived, yet?' The banquet was in the church basement and the main sanctuary was dark. When I went outside, there was Tony knocking on the door of the church. I introduced myself and took him downstairs to meet Phil. During the program, Phil asked Tony to sing, and he said he only knew one Christian song. I don't remember what the song was, but my wife, Mary Jean, accompanied him. From that moment on, history would be made."

Three thousand people jammed the Pasadena Civic Auditorium to hear the man many remembered from his "Cold, Cold Heart" days. None who attended that night suspected that the crooner of old would awe them with a voice and a delivery that only divine providence could have created, but that's what happened. Performing solo, and with Kerr and organist Les Barnett, Fontane instantly captivated his audience.

"I remember him vividly, as I was in the front row the night he was introduced to us and he gave his testimony," said Bill Burns, a high school student at the time. "I was worried for him, as he said he had been warned not to hit real high notes because of the injuries he had sustained in the accident, but he did so anyway."

Burns noted that Fontane appeared to know only a few songs and spent most of his time giving his testimony.

"I had to be brought to the brink of death before I would receive God's love and His Son, Jesus Christ, and let Him thaw out my cold, cold heart," Fontane said. "I hope that won't happen to you."

Burns recalled that "He gave the impression that it was all very new to him. It was one of those events that has always stayed with me."

The thunderous applause not only guaranteed the singer as many return engagements as he cared to make, but also signaled the beginning of one of the busiest careers in the gospel music industry.

Char first heard her father in a live performance several weeks after the first Monday Night Musical, and was amazed at Fontane's gift. "I didn't know he could sing like that," she said. "And the audience – It was as if God sprinkled magic dust over everyone. You could hear them sigh when he sang."

Not everyone, however, was charitable toward the Fontanes, probably because they didn't know of their recent plunge into poverty. At one Monday Night Musical, Kerry was criticized for wearing a glamorous formal dress.

"Little did they know," said Dean Brown, "that this was the only dress-up dress that Kerry had left, because of the lawsuit by Tony's agency."

Churches that once shunned Fontane now clamored for him, and Fontane rarely, if ever, turned down an invitation to sing and to share his testimony with the world.

"No fist-pounding oratory or revival tent fever prompted Fontane to dedicate his life to God, nor was that decision prompted by guilt or fear," noted a reporter for the *San Jose Mercury*. "Quite the contrary. He summarizes it simply: 'Christianity is faith in the heart. I'm not capable of hard-selling Christianity, but I can show through my life that it works.'"

In a further exploration of his approach to Christianity, Fontane told the *Mercury*:

"I refuse to get ridiculous or fanatical about religion. I'm not obliged, either, to tell a man, 'You're going to hell, brother,' because he'll know it if he is. I don't pack a New Testament around in my vest pocket, and I don't preach."

He didn't have to. His voice, and the story of his conversion, did his preaching for him. Kerr not only kept him performing at the Pasadena Civic Auditorium, but helped Fontane obtain bookings in churches, schools, and auditoriums across the country. Kerr even bought Fontane a reliable used car so that he could get to his bookings, and wrote a song for Fontane, "I'm In Love with the Lover of My Soul." It became one of Fontane's favorites.

"How I thank Jesus Christ for what He did for me in saving me and in giving me the assurance of eternal life," he told audiences just before singing Kerr's song. "I hope every one of you will enter into the joy and satisfaction of this perfect peace."

This "perfect peace" affected the entire dynamic of the Fontane household.

"Dad on average was a whole lot more mellow, although his patience level wasn't," said Char. "Mother became a wholly different person. In the past she had been a glass-of-wine here-and-there kind of person, sort of flirty with my Dad, but she became much more subdued and acted as an anchor for him. Her personality went from wild to peaceful, very centered."

The Fontane spiritual state may have been at peace, but little else was. A year after his near-fatal crash, Fontane still physically suffered from his injuries, and migraines plagued him regularly. His refusal to slow down – indeed, he increased his activity on a daily basis – undoubtedly exacerbated these physical ailments. Plus, he was mad to record again, and would find no peace until he had committed to vinyl the voice that God had restored to him. Toward that end, with Kerr on the piano and Les Barnett on the organ, Fontane cut an album with Los Angeles-based Cornerstone Records in late 1958. The title song, "I'm His To Command," was written by Kerr, and while the album's simplicity would later be overshadowed by much more spectacular recordings with full orchestration, *I'm His To Command* at least fulfilled Fontane's desire to record again.

Once again it was possible for people to carry the singer and his voice into their homes, and over the next sixteen years, untold millions of them would do so.

Chapter Eight

In 1959, as the story of his conversion became increasingly known in the Christian community, Fontane found himself so much in demand that he began to have difficulty balancing the responsibilities of his performance and recording schedules with those of his private life. Busy as he was, however, he did find time to take care of one very important personal commitment. Because he and Kerry had been married hurriedly by a judge during a lull in a murder trial nine years earlier, Fontane had promised that, one day, they would have a formal wedding ceremony. That day came on May 2, 1959, when the Fontanes exchanged their wedding vows anew in the forum that had given him his first break as a gospel singer, the Pasadena Civic Auditorium. The Reverend Phil Kerr performed the ceremony, seven-year-old Char was the flower girl, and three thousand people witnessed the ceremony in the auditorium. The photos taken of Fontane, resplendent in a tuxedo, and Kerry in full wedding gown, reveal two radiantly happy young people.

After recording *I'm His to Command,* Fontane quickly cut another record, this time with Christian Faith Recordings, a label founded in the early 1950s in Southern California. The *Tony Fontane, Lyric Tenor* album teamed him with pianist Rudy Atwood and his orchestra, and organist Les Barnett. The album's immediate success attracted the attention of executives at RCA Victor, who approached Fontane with an offer of a recording contract. While he would make some unsound business decisions later in his gospel career, Fontane struck gold when he accepted RCA's offer. The company would provide top-notch orchestration, production values, and marketing clout, all of which would propel Fontane into the stratosphere of the gospel-music industry. His first album for RCA, *The Touch of His Hand*, presaged the success that was to come. With the support of a full orchestra and a compelling corps of backup singers, Fontane gave a performance the likes of which he would not repeat in album form for the next fifteen years. He sang every song on the twelve-cut album as he would have done in his popular-music days at Mercury, crooning and texturing the songs with the kind of lilting playfulness that had made him a commercial success.

"Simply wonderful...that is how I feel after hearing Tony Fontane's first recordings for RCA Victor," noted film and television actress Dale Evans. "Here is a deeply devoted Christian young man who sings straight from the heart. I had the privilege of hearing his recordings before *The Touch of His Hand* was completed, and I truly believe millions of people throughout the world will experience a feeling of peace and joy after listening to this album."

As early as 1959, less than a year after he had embarked on his new life as a gospel singer, Fontane began to experience one of the business-related problems that would vex him for the rest of his career. When churches asked him to sing, the protocol was to take up an offering after the concert to pay Fontane for his time and expenses. But it sometimes didn't work that way. To be sure, churches took up the offering, but when it came time to count up the money, some of them were flabbergasted by how much cash lay in the collection plate. As a result, Fontane occasionally didn't get it all, which he knew, but didn't consider important enough to make an issue of.

"What do you want me to do?" he asked his wife and daughter. "I can't say I'm doing this for Christ and then demand money. God will give me what he thinks I will need."

Such was the state of affairs when Philadelphia native Billy Zeoli, director of the Indianapolis chapter of Youth for Christ, contacted Fontane and asked him to perform. Although the YFC movement was well known, having gotten its start in 1940 and established itself in Washington, D.C., Detroit, St. Louis, Indianapolis, and Chicago, Fontane told Zeoli he had to be paid up front.

"So I figured right away that someone hadn't given him his money," said the street-wise Zeoli. "I sent it to him, and he came, and the minute we met, it was like two guys who were brought up together."

Indeed. Fontane and Zeoli formed an instant and lasting friendship. Both were of Italian extraction with hardscrabble backgrounds, and both possessed a wickedly mischievous sense of humor – which, in a very short period of time, they were willing and eager to exert upon one another. The day they met, said Zeoli, they did nothing but laugh.

"He had a glow about him," Zeoli said of Fontane. "He walked into a room and you could look into his eyes and know the guy was mischief."

According to Zeoli, Fontane "knocked 'em flat" at the Youth for Christ concert the next day.

"Something spoke to my spirit and said, 'This guy is somebody that God wants you to help, just for a little while, to make sure somebody doesn't screw him up,'" Zeoli said. "So I did. I stayed with him."

Zeoli would be the closest thing to an agent that Fontane would tolerate during his gospel career. He booked the singer in concerts throughout the country and traveled with him by car and airplane from city to city, handling the set-ups and making sure Fontane got paid. One night, Zeoli experienced first-hand the gift-offering theft.

"I was walking through the back room where they were counting the offering, and they didn't see me," Zeoli said. "One guy said, 'Look at this – three one-thousand-dollar checks and a five-hundred-dollar check. We'd never get that much, ever, isn't that great?'

"Then I went out to where Tony was. The preacher came out to us and said, 'Dear boys, we're glad you're here. We had to add a little bit to the offering, but here it is, $750."

Zeoli advanced on the preacher, grabbed him by the arm, and drew back his fist. Fontane quickly stepped in and held Zeoli's arm while the preacher, the blood drained from his face, beat a hasty retreat.

"Just let it go," Fontane said.

"I tried to make him a businessman," Zeoli sighed, "but I was never able to."

A few years later, Fontane would explain his approach to money matters:

"I don't worry about money and don't set a blanket fee for

my church performances," he told a reporter. "I know I would be making a lot more money doing all this professionally, and I enjoyed making large sums of money. But it is personal conviction that Christ is a personal being, and that every man has his own decisions to make."

That incident aside, Zeoli said he most remembers two elements of touring with Tony Fontane: the humor, and the powerful effect Fontane's singing had on the audiences he performed for.

Zeoli noted that one of Fontane's most famous pranks centered on his uncanny ability to mimic the cry of a kitten in distress, and to throw his voice so that no one knew where the sound originated.

One day, aboard an Air Canada flight, Fontane occupied a seat in the fourth row while Zeoli was seated in the sixteenth row. As the plane sat on the tarmac waiting to take off, Zeoli heard the familiar kitten-cry. Deciding to aid and abet Fontane in the joke, Zeoli started sneezing and coughing, telling a stewardess he was allergic to cats.

"That cat is about to kill me," he said. "Can you get a doctor?"

While a doctor was being sent for, Fontane – who had thrown the kitten cry several more times and had the entire plane looking for it – decided to irritate an unfriendly Brit in the seat next to him.

"The kitten is in that man's briefcase, I just know it," Fontane whispered to the stewardess. "Make him open it."

"The English guy got real mad," said Zeoli, "but he did it."

Then, Zeoli told the stewardess that they could coax the kitten into the open by placing a saucer of milk in the aisle. Although the milk was laid, and an entire planeload of people coaxed with multiples of "kitty, kitty, kitty," the feline, naturally, never appeared.

"We had to end this thing somehow and get to the next city," said Zeoli. "The plane was already twelve minutes late taking off. The cat had quit meowing, I told the doctor I felt better, and so the plane took off.

"About a thousand feet off the ground, you hear this, 'meow,

meow.' It drove everybody nuts, but nobody ever found that kitten. Nobody ever caught on. Tony could look at you with a straight face and look so innocent."

Fontane's daughter said many years later that her father also performed the kitten-in-distress stunt in restaurants, department stores, public places of all kinds, even churches, frequently emptying them as people searched for the crying feline.

"He could stand right beside you and throw his voice, and you'd never know it was him," said Char. " He thought it was hilarious. It drove my mother nuts."

Fontane, commenting on his enjoyment of life, once said, "If I couldn't smile, I wouldn't want to be a Christian. I was miserable without God, why should I be miserable with him?"

Zeoli had his moments, as well. In a Des Moines, Iowa, hotel just prior to a concert, Fontane had allowed his temper to get the better of him, and was ranting about a publicity mix-up.

"He was Italian, and blew his stack a lot, especially at inefficiency," Zeoli said.

On this occasion, Fontane got out of the shower and walked into the hotel room he and Zeoli shared, completely naked, still ranting. Suddenly, Zeoli snapped open the hotel room door and shoved Fontane into the hallway. He slammed the door shut and locked it.

There was a second doorway to the room just down the hall, so the naked Fontane made a dash for it. Zeoli got there just ahead of him, and locked that door, as well. Then, Zeoli went back to the first door, opened it, stuck his head into the hallway and shouted, "Hey, Tony!" When Fontane made a break for the open door, Zeoli closed and locked it. This happened several more times, with the nude singer racing up and down the hallway trying to get inside his room.

Fontane pleaded with Zeoli to let him in, but Zeoli just laughed through the locked doors. When Fontane heard the hotel's elevator coming to a stop, he became frantic.

"I'll never get mad again," he promised. "I'll buy you all the spaghetti in the world….anything…just let me in."

Just before the elevator doors opened and passengers stepped into the hallway, said Zeoli, he let Fontane in.

November 4, 1922, wedding photo of Raphaela and Joseph Trankina. The couple married over the strong objections of her family. Their second son, Tony Fontane, was born in a railroad box car in Ann Arbor, Michigan.

Above, a teenaged Tony Trankina scowls at the camera in North Dakota.

Below, Fontane as a member of the U.S. Coast Guard, in which he served for the duration of World War II.

Fontane sings in an undated, unidentified television appearance. He was a frequent performer on many of the top shows of the late 1940s and early 1950s.

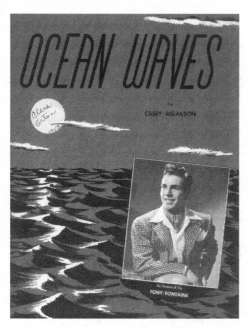

Left: Sheet music from the early 1950s for "Ocean Waves," a song recorded by Tony Fontane. The song was written in 1929 by Casey Aslakson and typifed the type of music performed by Fontane at the height of his popular career.

Right: Fontane graces the cover of the April 14, 1951, edition of *TV Forecast*.

In both the sheet music and the *TV Forecast*, Fontane's name was spelled "Fontaine" -- an error that happened frequently through-out his career

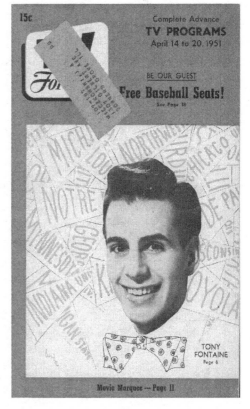

Above: Kerry, Char'ae and Tony Fontane are captured by a newspaper photographer at a San Jose, California, soda fountain.

Left: A scene from *The Tony Fontane Story.*

Above: Tony, Char'ae and Kerry Fontane on a trip to the Holy Land.

Below: Fontane poses beside a Cessna given to him by an admirer.

Fontane in a studio
recording session.

The marquee at the
Municipal Audito-
rium in Pasadena,
California, advertises
a Tony Fontane con-
cert. He performed
here frequently.

Left: Fontane publicity photo, circa 1965. Right, Kerry Fontane in a glamor shot while on the set of *The Tony Fontane
Story.*

Advertisement for Fontane's film, *God's Country.* The movie is now cosidered lost.

"Tony never got scared," he said with a laugh, "but he was scared that time."

But Zeoli also remembers how Fontane's performances all over the country were often emotionally moving events. At one massive venue in the Midwest, Fontane finished singing and Zeoli offered a prayer. Fontane then stepped up to the microphone and began asking people to come to the front to accept Christ.

"They came by the hundreds," Zeoli said. "Tony started weeping, and he couldn't go on. He cried and cried, and kept saying how good God was to a jerk like him. I dealt with the people, while he cried. He just couldn't get over it, how good God was to a jerk like him."

In 1959, Fontane was a featured performer at the annual Youth for Christ convention at Winona Lake, Indiana. He sang one of his most requested numbers, Stuart Hamblin's "Until Then," giving it the crooner treatment to an elaborate piano accompaniment. At the conclusion, YFC leader Ted Engstrom said, "What a marvelous trophy of God's grace," and in a prayer before the sermon, musician Ted Roe noted, "We have already seen and heard a sermon."

Fontane and Zeoli also enjoyed providing unscheduled public performances. In Denver, the pair went to an Italian restaurant that featured a three-piece band and singing waiters. Zeoli entered the restaurant first and found the manager. He shoved a couple of Fontane's albums at him and said, "You see the man on these albums? He's going to come in here for dinner. I don't want you to let people know he's here. Do you understand that?"

It was, Zeoli admitted with a chuckle, his way of building up the singer's name value and, at the same time, setting the stage for an impromptu Fontane performance. The buildup probably wasn't necessary, for when Fontane walked into the restaurant and shook hands with the manager, his charm and magnetic personality captivated the restaurateur. The manager looked at the polished, handsome singer, glanced at one of the albums in his hand, and said, "Wow, that must be some album."

After dinner, Zeoli again went to the manager and said, "Because of your thoughtfulness and kindness, I'm going to have Tony do one song for you," a proposition to which the manager quickly agreed. The song, Zeoli announced to the restaurant, was Elvis Presley's recent number-one hit, "It's Now or Never," which employed the melody of the nineteenth century Neapolitan song, "O Solo Mio." But the tune had yet another incarnation as a 1921 inspirational song titled "Down From His Glory," and it was this version, rich in Christian message, that Zeoli and Fontane ultimately wanted the audience to hear.

The three-piece band struck up the notes to "It's Now Or Never," and Fontane gave the audience what it wanted – the Elvis Presley version, without, in all probability, the King of Rock 'n Roll's signature hip swinging. Then he sang it again, as "O Solo Mio," in Italian. After each version, the audience responded with warm applause. Then, Fontane told the band to play it again, and he sang the song as "Down From His Glory." Finally, for Fontane, the version that meant something. He threw his heart and soul and every measure of the powerful new voice God had given him into the song.

"When it was over, the restaurant went nuts," Zeoli said. "You couldn't hear yourself think for all the applause and the shouting."

The message had been delivered. Zeoli also acknowledged that the incident – and many others similar to it all over the country – hadn't done any harm to Fontane's growing popularity.

In December of 1959, another impromptu performance literally stopped people in their tracks. Fontane was in Chicago, accompanying a group of several hundred Youth for Christ devotees on their way to Washington, D.C., for a convention. These conventioneers, plus hundreds of other travelers, jammed Union Station. Without planning or prompting, Fontane positioned himself on a balcony overlooking the spacious, marbled expanse below, and began to sing. Without a microphone, Fontane let the natural power of his voice fill the station as he sang "God of the Mountain." Below, the hundreds of travelers came to a stop, looked up at Fontane, and listened, transfixed. After the final notes passed away into the vaulted expanses of the station, the crowd below Fontane erupted into applause.

"It was a significant moment," said Rick McLain, an eyewitness to the event.

The price of Fontane's growing popularity was high. Between 1959 and 1960, Fontane logged 168,000 air miles as he met concert commitments in churches, auditoriums, schools, college campuses, meeting halls and theaters in every state of the Union. Additionally, the first Sunday of every month found him performing a Christian concert series in Pittsburgh's Carnegie Music Hall. In a June 4, 1960, feature story about Fontane, the *San Jose Mercury* commented on his brutal performance schedule:

> Following a Friday night engagement in San Jose, he boarded a jet airliner for Houston, Tex., where he attended a conference of the International Union of Missions and Churches. His schedule returns him here for a 7 p.m. engagement Sunday when the First Baptist Church moves the Fontane-(Merv) Rosell citywide crusade to Civic Auditorium.
>
> The energy demand of Fontane's continent-hopping itinerary doesn't seem to tax his vigor.

Appearances, however, were deceiving.

"Tony never fully recovered from the severe injuries he had sustained in the car accident that originally brought him to Christ," said Dean Brown of the Monday Night Musicals. "His health remained very fragile and he was in pain almost constantly. In fact, when Phil Kerr died in 1960, the family wanted Tony to sing at the funeral, but he was on the East Coast and very ill at the time himself, and was unable to attend."

And yet, he pushed himself, both professionally and personally. After a performance in Toledo, Ohio, Fontane insisted that he and Zeoli drive to Grand Rapids, Michigan, to see Zeoli's oldest boy, Steve, in a play at church.

"The kid had three lines," Zeoli said. "But we packed up, got in my car, and took off for Grand Rapids, just so Tony could see Steve in his play. Three lines. Drove all night long just for three lines."

The demands on Fontane's time, talent and stamina weren't going to get any better any time soon. In fact, an idea conceived by Zeoli in one of the many hotel waysides he and Fontane shared would soon push the singer to even more challenging levels, and would result in the most spectacular success any gospel singer had achieved to that point.

First, though, Fontane had to face another yet desperate, life-threatening situation. In February of 1961, just when the lives, finances and personal fulfillments of the Fontanes were rising, tragedy struck. Kerry, who had been ill for some time, was diagnosed with advanced cervical cancer. The word from her doctors was devastating: Kerry Fontane had no more than eight weeks to live. There was nothing medically that could be done for her.

Fontane was crushed. In a reversal of the scenario that had played itself out just four years earlier with his automobile accident, he now lived at the bedside of his wife, who had been admitted to the UCLA Medical Center. As the weeks went by, he watched her lose weight until she became a frail shadow of her former self. Although he prayed nearly without letup, there was no discernible change in Kerry's condition. When it was suggested to him that he allow faith healers to have a go at it, Fontane jumped at the offer. After all, even though medical science had helped pull him through his own brush with death, wasn't his survival also a miracle of faith?

"A small group of people came to the hospital and collected in a circle around her bed," Char recalled. "A woman – I don't remember her name – began to pray over her, slowly, slowly, slowly. She reached out and touched my mother, laid hands on her, while the entire group prayed. They came back day after day and did this, for hours at a time, while my father and I watched and prayed with them."

UCLA's doctors were, understandably, skeptical. Faith healing was something completely outside their realm of experience, expertise and scope of credibility. They were flabbergasted when, slowly, Kerry Fontane began to recover without a scintilla of medical treatment. As the weeks passed, she gained back her weight and her strength. New tests revealed that her cancer was in remission and, within several months, had disappeared altogether.

"Every year for the rest of her life, the doctor at UCLA would send her the funniest letter," said Char. "It would say, 'Dear Kerry Fontane, are you still alive?' He simply couldn't imagine how this miracle had occurred."

Char also noted that the experience worked a change in Kerry herself. From that time on, she, too, seemed to have the ability to heal through the laying on of hands.

"My mother was in a service with my father about six months after she started getting better," Char said. "A little boy ran up to her at the alter call, and the boy's mother said 'My son is sick, and he seems to think you could pray over him.' So she prayed over him, and put her hands on him, and she got this feeling through her fingers, like a warmth and an energy. The boy got better instantly."

Kerry repeated the procedure often after that, healing children who were sometimes deathly ill. One time, though, the very sick child she laid hands on didn't get better. Kerry, said Char, was very angry with God about it.

"My father sat her down and explained to her that now was the time she needed to stop, because she had begun to think that it was her doing, not God's," Char remembered. "She said, 'You're right. He was using me as a vessel,' and from that time on she backed off, and let the example of the miracle that had been worked on her stand on its own merit."

Chapter Nine

In 1959, Tony Fontane and Billy Zeoli sat in one of the countless hotel rooms that were an integral part of their lives on the road and focused on what each of them did best. Fontane practiced for the concert he would give that night, fretted over details of the performance, and looked ahead to upcoming appearances in other cities. Zeoli bounced ideas around in his head.

It struck him like a battering ram. He looked at Fontane. Standing there, going over his music, was the embodiment of perhaps the single most inspirational story Zeoli had ever heard. Here was a man who had been a popular recording artist, a rich and glittering entertainment figure, and an atheist who had nearly lost his life in a devastating car crash. Here was a man who had found Christ, turned his back on his secular pursuits, and who was now becoming the country's most popular gospel singer. If it hadn't been a true story, no one would have believed it. The man's survival was a miracle, and the message his life represented underscored the greatest miracle of them all – salvation and redemption for even the most callous of disbelievers.

It would make a great movie, thought Zeoli. Fontane would, of course, play himself. After all, who other than Fontane could deliver that potent, clarion tenor voice? Kerry could portray herself, and Char…The idea quickly took shape, but when Zeoli proposed it to Fontane, the singer was dubious. A seasoned entertainer, he knew that films required money, writers, directors, technical crews, and backing in myriad crucial ways. But Zeoli was fired up, and he got Fontane fired up, as well, using two arguments to make his case.

First, he said, Fontane's performance schedule verged on the grotesque, with the singer knocking out as many as seven concerts or church services in a day. He traveled three hundred fifty days a year and had even begun to reach beyond the borders of the United States. In a recent tour to South America, more than twenty thousand people had heard Fontane sing at one concert, and that with only two days' notice.

"The human body, no matter how dedicated, can only stand so much stress and strain, can only be one place at a time, can speak and sing a limited number of times in a day," Zeoli said.

The answer? A movie that would spread the Gospel through the life and testimony of Tony Fontane.

Zeoli's second argument was that he had an inside track to a non-profit ministry called Gospel Films. In the early 1950s, Zeoli had assumed the presidency of the company, the mission of which was to use film to communicate the Christian message. He proposed that he and Fontane take the idea to the company's board and see what happened. Fontane agreed.

"I knew our board of directors didn't want to make a film about a guy who was still alive," Zeoli said. "So we didn't mention the movie idea to them right away. I had Tony come before the board and sing. After he sang, I said, 'Tony, tell your testimony,' and he told them with tears in his eyes."

By the time Fontane had finished, Zeoli was trying to find a way to broach the topic of making a movie about his life. Before he could say a word, no fewer than six board members blurted out, "That's our next film!"

The Tony Fontane Story was born, and Christian entertainment history was about to be made.

Many elements had to fall into place before the first frame of film could be shot. Executive producer Zeoli and star Fontane tapped into every personal and professional resource they had in order to raise money for the project, the production of which would be turned over to Youth Films, the teenage division of Gospel Films.

"One of the most thrilling testimonies of this century , combined with the common language of music, will give this film a future ministry that will privilege literally millions of people with the clarity of the Gospel of Christ," Zeoli wrote in a promotional piece designed to raise money for the movie. The dollars poured in, and the project got under way.

Jan Sadlo, a young director of Christian films and animated television features, was tapped to direct. The cast would include Fontane and Kerry as themselves, and Char would snag two roles. In a flashback scene, she would portray her father as a boy growing up in the mission and, later, she would portray herself.

Fontane assumed the task of writing the script. He significantly consolidated many areas of his life and completely ignored others, so that in the end, the script actually generated more questions about his background than it answered. Other components were dramatized to the point of fictionalization, such as the sudden and miraculous recovery of his voice following a single prayer, and yet others were invented out of whole cloth for entertainment value. Interestingly, he omitted the faith healing element of his wife's miracle cure, and focused instead on the sole curative power of God. Holding it all together as factual, though, was the storyline that Tony Fontane, hotshot entertainer and avowed atheist, had found God thanks to a life-threatening car crash, and had turned his life into a crusade for Christ. Other parts of the script, such as one in which Char asks her father about performing in Las Vegas – "What would you do if Jesus walked in?" – came straight out of real life, as did Kerry's bedside prayer for the life of her husband.

It took Fontane and Zeoli two and a half years to pull all the pieces together, but in late 1961, in Los Angeles, filming finally began. Cast and crew members stayed at the De Soto Hotel and worked for eleven weeks to shoot exteriors and interiors. Additional filming was completed in New York and in Gospel Films' new studio in Muskegon, Michigan, and some even took place on the road with Fontane, who, incredibly, maintained his concert schedule during filming.

"I controlled the film, script, content, how it went, where the gospel was, or where it wasn't," Zeoli said. "If Tony had a song that wasn't right, nobody would tell him. I'd have to call him over to the side and say, 'We can do better.'"

Zeoli said Fontane seemed to have no qualms about re-enacting the car accident that had nearly killed him and, to that day, provided him with unremitting pain. Char, looking back on the making of *The Tony Fontane Story*, marveled that her father was psychologically able to recreate the event.

"It was something he never talked about, never even referred

89

to, except when he gave his testimony in concerts," she said. "He did everything he could to block it from his mind."

Char's experience with the making of the film was mixed.

"I was born aspiring to act," she said. "There was nothing else I ever wanted to do. But, oh…I hated playing the role of my father as a boy in the early part of the film. I was so embarrassed. To play a boy….I was just mortified."

She admitted that, at the ripe old age of nine, she thought of herself as the consummate actress, one who knew far more about the craft than her entertainer father.

"I remember once he said to me, 'Turn your head when you say that line and look at me,' and I thought, 'That really doesn't look good,' and did it my own way. We did about eleven takes, and he finally took my chin in his hand and said, 'Do you understand? This is turning your head.' Of course, I was mortified in front of the cast and crew, so I did what he wanted and turned my head. It was a good lesson I learned about direction."

Char also remembers one particularly moving moment during the making of the movie. A scene unfolds in which Kerry kneels beside the hospital bed of the critically injured Fontane, and prays for his recovery.

"It was the only part of the film where I saw her not act," Char said. "Before she met my father, she hadn't led a perfect life, and when, in the scene, she said, 'Please, Jesus, I've done so many terrible things,' and started to cry – well, there was no acting going on there. It was real. She ended up crying for an hour after we shot it. My mother had to fight the remorse she felt for many, many years, even though she knew she was forgiven. It was the most honest moment they captured in that film."

Dan Friberg, a young trumpeter who often played at the Monday Night Musicals, remembered being booked with Fontane at an Orange County Youth for Christ Rally.

"When I arrived, I saw trucks, and people walking around hurriedly, and didn't know what to think," said Friberg, of Fontana, California. "When I got inside the church, I saw Tony and asked him what was going on. He said, 'After the service, we're shooting a scene for my movie. Why don't you stick around and be in it?'

"Well," continued Friberg, "he didn't have to ask me twice. In the movie, there's a scene where, after a concert, there are young people surrounding Tony. There is one young person standing next to Tony – me! – with an album, who asks Tony to autograph it. My one brief shining moment!"

Edited by Cordell Fray, *The Tony Fontane Story* went into the can and was scheduled for mass release in the fall of 1962. In the interim, Fontane continued his non-stop concert schedule, while Zeoli concentrated on generating publicity for the upcoming film. Interest in the Christian community abounded as Zeoli saturated the media with magazine and newspaper articles, brochures, advertisements and promotional appearances. Of course, Fontane himself promoted the movie in all his concerts, and by the time it was released in September of 1962, his fans were eager to patronize it.

The Tony Fontane Story was unique in two ways. It was the first full-color, Christian dramatic musical ever produced, and not a penny of admission or usage fees were ever charged for its showing. It was offered free to thousands of venues across the country, including movie theaters, television stations, high schools, churches, civic groups – anyone who wanted to show it. The ever-energetic Zeoli also made sure copies of the movie, dubbed into different languages, were distributed to eighty foreign countries in which Gospel Films operated.

Neither Fontane nor Zeoli were fully prepared for the overwhelming success of the movie around the globe. Tens of thousands of churches, packed to the rafters with people, showed the film several times a day for days at a time. When churches couldn't accommodate the crowds, movie theaters and auditoriums were rented, and they, too, were jammed. Across the nation, hundreds of thousands of people were saved because of the message they saw on the screen. Zeoli's vision of the Fontane ministry reaching out beyond the singer's physical capabilities was coming to fruition.

Retired high-school principal Steve Carlton, who was a sixteen-year-old Ohio high-school student at the time of the film's release, was a case in point.

"I had been invited by a friend to attend a Youth for Christ rally in Dayton," said Carlton, of Encinitas, California. "I really had no interest in spiritual things, but there was a nudge in my heart to go, so I agreed. That night, *The Tony Fontane Story* was shown to an auditorium full of young people, and when the invitation was given to receive Christ and commit our lives to serving Jesus, dozens of teenagers walked forward.

"Although I was too shy to go forward," he went on, "God continued to speak to me throughout the evening, and that night at my bedside, I knelt and asked Jesus to come into my heart and forgive me and be my Lord and Savior from that moment on. Tony's story of grace and transformation led me to Christ, and I am eternally thankful that God used him to plant the seed that has grown to faith and service."

One of the Spanish-language versions of the movie, shown in the Cuban communities in Florida, generated this comment from a pastor there: "Through two prints of your film, we have reached thousands of Cuban refugees in Florida. Already there are 2,137 of these who have accepted Christ as savior in the past six months."

Overseas, the movie was having a similar impact. Zeoli received hundreds of letters from missionaries who had shown the film and who attested to its power.

"I have preached to over twenty thousand different people because of your film," wrote a missionary in Thailand. "Without your film, I might have contacted one thousand."

Another missionary, in Aba, Nigeria, wrote: "I intended to give you an exact account of the number in each service, but the crowds to see your film were so large that it was never possible to count them."

Fontane frequently traveled with the movie, singing and interacting with crowds, and selling and signing records afterwards. Zeoli recalled an incident that was amusing from two standpoints: that Fontane still retained his temper, and that he could be put into his place by someone even more volatile than himself.

It happened at a large auditorium in Lansing, Michigan.

Every seat was filled and people lined up outside for admittance to the next show. Unfortunately, a 35-millimeter projector was used to show the 16-millimeter film.

"On the screen, Tony looked like he was about three feet tall," said Zeoli. "Backstage, he started to fume. Inefficiency of any kind just got under his skin."

The film was quickly stopped, and a compatible projector was brought into service. This time, however, the operators couldn't get the film focused. Fontane, steaming, began to complain bitterly.

Zeoli's father, an old-time Mafia gangster who had abandoned his hardscrabble life of crime for one as an evangelist, was present. He walked up to Fontane, grabbed him by the arm and said, "Listen, you bum, you deserve to go to hell. That's where you belong. You control your mouth; people make mistakes."

Fontane, instantly subdued, blinked down at the tough old man and said, respectfully, "Yes, sir."

The Tony Fontane Story played, without letup and without any reduction in its value as a Christian outreach tool, for years. It netted Fontane vast television, radio and newspaper coverage, and helped promote record sales, as well, particularly an album that featured songs from the movie. In 1963, for the first time in the history of the National Evangelical Film Foundation, all major awards went to *The Tony Fontane Story*. It was named outstanding film of the year. Tony and Kerry received outstanding actor and actress of the year awards. Zeoli snagged producer of the year, and Sadlo was named director of the year. To boot, the album spawned by the movie, *Songs from The Tony Fontane Story,* was voted outstanding record of the year.

Viewed from a distance, *The Tony Fontane Story* is very dated. While production values were good for its time, improved filmmaking techniques have made it, today, a technological curiosity piece. The acting is, in many cases, marginal – Fontane, said Char, admitted he wasn't an actor, but had a good time doing it – and some of the situations are painfully corny. It is at times impossible to suspend disbelief, such as in a scene that has Fontane whipping up an impromptu orchestral arrangement out of thin air for one of the many songs in the film. The average twenty-first century viewer will find much of the content improbable, even laughable, in places.

Not laughable, however, are the dynamic performances of Tony Fontane throughout the movie. His rendition of "The Lord's Prayer," for example, still has the power to send chill bumps exploding along the spine. He reaches the final soaring notes of the song, and just when it seems he can't go any higher, he does, and holds it, for one of the most dramatic conclusions to an inspirational song ever recorded. "Peace Like A River," on the other hand, is smooth, lilting and soulful, and gives the listener a hint of the crooner that once was. "My Jesus, I Love Thee," sung at his cancer-stricken wife's bedside, is soft, and controlled, and poignant. While the movie about Tony Fontane has not stood the test of time particularly well, the album it generated has, and remains one of Fontane's best and most popular productions. The album ranked first in the religious field on the West Coast, and was awarded a four-star rating by Variety magazine.

The message, too, remains. People who saw the movie in the early 1960s and who reviewed it for the first time more than forty-five years later quickly looked past the acting, the fading color and the improbable situations. What they saw, and what struck them with visceral potency, was the story of hope and salvation that Tony Fontane's life, thanks to a merciful God, exemplified. And for Fontane, and Zeoli, and all who were associated with the making of the movie, that was the only real mission.

Chapter Ten

Even though Tony Fontane abandoned his mainstream, secular career, he never turned his back on the many show business luminaries who had become his friends in his pre-Christian days. He and John Wayne were, according to Char, "two peas in a pod" who loved to talk politics (both were staunch conservatives) and joke with one another at every opportunity.

"They had exactly the same Christian and political beliefs," Char said. "That was the very private part of Wayne's life. He wasn't a born-again Christian as you would normally think of one, but he was very strong in his faith. He said exactly what he thought and so did my father, so they got along famously."

Sammy Davis, Jr., was an acquaintance, as was Frank Sinatra, Rosemary Clooney, Jack Palance and Steve Allen. Scores of other film, radio, television and music industry icons numbered among Fontane's acquaintances.

"They were his people, and he knew how to talk to them," said Char. "He could tell them about his conversion and what it meant to him, and witness to them about their own spiritual well-being, without coming across as being pushy or dogmatic. That wouldn't have gotten anywhere with the likes of John Wayne or Frank Sinatra. Most of them loved my father, and enjoyed being around him, whether or not they decided to make any spiritual changes in their lives."

Fontane seemed comfortable with the balance in his life of showbiz friendships and Christianity.

"Some of them can't accept the faith I have found and I try to share that faith with them," he said. "But up until ten years ago I called myself an atheist, so I don't look down my nose at people who have not yet found the joy I find in Christ."

But it was the ordinary, workaday folk with whom Fontane spent the greater portion of his time and whose company he seemed to most enjoy. Although he presented a glamorous image – crisp suits, expensive jewelry, imported sports cars, rivers of Woodhue cologne – he never forgot the poverty and deprivations of his youth, and as a result mingled easily with the moms and pops who made up his fan base. Indeed, Fontane seemed to go out of his way to cultivate their friendships and, even, to make himself a part of their lives. Few were reluctant to let him do so, for the same charm and humor that made him a favorite among Hollywood's elite also delighted middle-class Americans everywhere. Also, thousands of Fontane's public appearances were in small or mid-sized towns and cities, and so it was the middle-class backbone of America with whom he most often came into contact. Many times, instead of bunking in a hotel, Fontane would stay with people who opened their homes to him.

Dr. and Mrs. Chet Strehlow of Ottawa, Kansas, frequently hosted special guests at the Kansas City Youth for Christ rallies, and in early 1964 provided hospitality to Fontane following one of the crusades there. The couple offered to take all five of their children, with Fontane, to Ottawa's best restaurant, the L&L Café. Four-year-old David Strehlow, however, put up such a fuss that his parents hired a baby sitter for the evening, and then went out to enjoy the company of Tony Fontane.

"Well, after an hour of being away from the family and the ever-charming Tony, I convinced my baby sitter to call my mother at the café," said Strehlow, who went on to become senior pastor at Liberty Hills Baptist Church in Liberty, Missouri. "Within minutes, I was whisked away in my pajamas to be seated to Tony's immediate left in the booth at the café. I salivated as I saw him carving on a thick, juicy steak, cooked just like I liked it!"

Fontane, said Strehlow, sensed his bashfulness, and talked to him in warm, endearing terms.

"As I looked up into his handsome, dimple-chinned face, he smiled and said, 'Here, have a piece of my steak.' It couldn't have made me feel more special."

Fontane continued to spend time with the Strehlows when he passed through the area. David Strehlow remembers him stretching a handkerchief over his hand to form a puppet, and then throwing his voice to make the puppet come alive.

"I will never forget the short time that I was able to spend in close range to this wonderful Christian man," he said.

At about the same time, Bud Cole, of Ohio, was staying in a Louisville, Kentucky, motel room when he saw on a local television channel an interview with Fontane, who also sang a song. That evening Cole, deeply impressed with what he had heard, attended Fontane's concert.

"A packed house sat spellbound for about two hours," Cole said. "I returned to my home in Ohio and told my wife about this fantastic voice. We agreed to drive almost three hours the next day to hear him again. Never have I heard such a voice singing Christian songs."

After the performance, the couple stopped at a nearby restaurant for a sandwich.

"Would you believe it, in came Mr. Fontane and a few others and sat in the booth next to us," Cole said. "Well, my wife and I said hello, and he invited us to join them. In no time I felt we had known each other for years. My wife requested a special song for the next evening's service, and he said he would see what he could do."

The next night, Fontane "preached a little and sang a lot," and then, to the surprise of the Coles, said, "This song is for Mary Ellen Cole, one of my newest friends."

"How blessed we were," Cole said. "I still focus on his voice when I hear him over the radio today, and say I was blessed to know him and call him friend."

Fontane, who was an accomplished cook, loved to prepare elaborate Italian dinners in the homes of the people he stayed with. Despite his pain and bone-crushing weariness, would sit up half the night talking and sharing with folks stories from his Hollywood days. Paul Meco recalled that, when Fontane stayed with his family in Pittsburgh, he once shared with them the best compliment he had ever received.

"The mother of Mario Lanza attended one of his concerts and, afterwards, told him, 'Tony, you sing just like my Mario,'" said Meco.

Not everyone was enchanted with Fontane, however. His success and attraction to outward signs of success put some people off. But thanks to his quick wit and innate toughness,

Fontane was up to the challenge. At one church, a woman walked up to him, leaned forward, and sniffed.

"You are obviously wearing perfume," she said disdainfully.

Fontane quickly leaned toward the woman, sniffed, and said, "And you, madam, obviously are not."

Some Christians were put off because Fontane refused to adopt a particular denomination, but he responded to them by saying, "It's not the label, it's what's in the can."

Others scoffed at his penchant for flashy clothes. Fontane would retort, "God didn't change my wardrobe. He changed my heart."

An article in the *Wisconsin State Journal* explored Fontane's take on worldly delights and the Christian life:

> Another interesting fact about Fontane is that, though he says he has committed his soul to Christ, that fact doesn't mean he has committed his personality to the narrow rigidity which characterizes much of the conservative church.
>
> Fontane is, in a word, flamboyant. Interviewed at the National Motor Inn where he was staying, Fontane appeared dressed in varying shades of maroon with a color coordinated watch and a solid gold lion's head ring on his finger. Learning that one of the hotel restaurant waitresses was celebrating her 19th anniversary, he kissed her soundly.
>
> If the above leads you to write Fontane a nasty letter explaining that he is really a demon in angel's clothing (red plastic shoes?), you will be one of the few thousand persons a year who do so.
>
> "I don't think the fact that the Lord let me become a Christian means that the Lord wants me to walk around looking dour and rejecting life," he said. "In fact, I think the fact I have become a Christian gives me something to be happy about. I'm happier than I have ever been."

A large part of his happiness lay in his marriage to Kerry. They appeared to be polar opposites – he hot-tempered, virile, and emotional, and she cool, aloof and in control – but the pairing worked extraordinarily well. Kerry never seemed to resent Fontane's three-hundred-fifty-day-a-year performance and touring schedule and, when he was at home, never complained when he shut himself up in his study for long hours of writing, reading or thinking.

"He's doing what he needs to do," Kerry told Char one day. "Leave him alone."

Char remembers when, as a child, she would walk into her parents' bedroom first thing in the morning and find them lying there, having just awakened.

"She'd be like a child, with my father holding her with her head on his shoulder and stroking her hair," she said. "I always thought, 'That's so nice, I hope I can get that one day.' They loved each other deeply."

Which was fortunate, because despite his prominence as a gospel singer and devout Christian, women made advances towards him or, worse, showed up at the Fontanes' front door claiming that the singer had promised to run away with them. Kerry would just say, "We're not buying, good-bye," and close the door, knowing that Fontane was innocent.

"My mother was so sure of herself that Brigitte Bardot could have walked in naked and she wouldn't have cared, because she knew that my father adored her," Char said. "She had it over everybody else. I, on the other hand, was extremely possessive of my dad."

Char's possessiveness demonstrated itself in a dramatic way at the Santa Monica Civic Hall where Fontane was singing. An attractive brunette was on the stage flirting with Fontane, while Char sat in the fifth row watching and fuming.

"She was tittering, and touching him, and my dad was smiling at her and being his usual charming self," said Char. "Mom said, 'Oh, Char, he smiles at everybody, he doesn't even care. You've got to get over this.'"

"Okay," said Char, but when Kerry went to the bathroom and the flirtatious brunette walked down from the stage and into the aisle, Char, who was sitting in the aisle seat, jammed her leg out. The woman tripped and fell flat on her face.

Picking herself up, the woman said, "I guess you didn't see me," to which Char replied, "Oh, yes I did."

"My father – I saw him up on the stage – tried to be angry with me, but he was laughing so hard he had tears in his eyes," she said. "I once asked him about the come-ons of women, and suggested that surely he was tempted. He said, 'Not ever.' I asked him why, and he said, 'When I have steak at home, why would I ever go for hamburger?'"

When Char said, "Yeah, but...," Fontane responded, "There are no buts. I got what I dreamed of. Why would I jeopardize that for a moment? I've got the best."

While Fontane's life had pivoted one hundred eighty degrees since his conversion to Christianity, that one tenet – his rock-solid fidelity to his wife and family – remained constant.

He loved animals, surrounding himself at home with cats and dogs. Char noted that "when you're attacked a lot, as he was, he just liked to shut himself up with dogs and their unconditional love." Once, on a hunting trip to Alaska, he saw a grizzly bear shot and skinned.

"He said he had never seen anything that looked like a human man so much as a bear skinned," said Char. "He never went hunting again."

At times, Fontane seemed to lead a charmed life. In the mid 1960s, he was in Florida for an engagement, after which he was to fly home to be with Kerry and Char.

"We were sitting around the house waiting to hear from him, to tell us when we could pick him up," Char recalled. "We were watching television, and suddenly a news report came on about the crash of the flight my father was on, and the death of everyone on board. Mom and I were hysterical."

All attempts to get through to the airline were fruitless. Kerry, said Char, was "in a heap." Five hours later the telephone rang. On the other end of the line was Fontane, who hadn't heard a thing about the crash of his flight.

"I met this guy at the airport and he really needed to hear about Jesus," said Fontane. "I hope you don't mind, but I cancelled my flight and decided to take the one after it. It was more important."

The incident, said Char, "knocked the wind out of me." She and her mother wept for hours.

The relationship between Fontane and his daughter was, in many respects, not unlike those of parents and children everywhere. While Fontane wasn't much of a disciplinarian, Char was rebellious, anyway, and later admitted to being headstrong and overly confident of her own knowledge and abilities. She disdained much of her father's advice and insisted, frequently, on following her own course. Sometimes, it backfired on her, in very public places.

Char and her father were in a restaurant when the teenaged Char, made up to look much older than her years, was smitten with one of the waiters. She began to "make eyes" at him, and decided she was "madly in love with him." Fontane saw what was going on and warned her.

"You do not understand what this man thinks," he told her. "He thinks you're older."

She ignored her father and continued to flirt with the waiter. When the waiter came back over to the table, Fontane said to him, "I want you to show my daughter pictures of your wife and children, because she thinks she's in love with you."

"I thought I was going to die of embarrassment," said Char. "But, it was such a good thing to do, because I could have gotten into some deep trouble. He was very protective of me."

He was indulgent, as well. When Char became a devoted fan of child actress Hailey Mills, Fontane booked a flight for Hollywood, found the Mills home, and took his daughter to meet the young actress, "just because I wanted it," she said.

Fontane also did all he could to help Char realize her dream of becoming an actress. He and Kerry allowed her to audition for all the popular television shows of the day, and supported her when she got the roles. When she formed her own small band, Kaci and the Undertakers, he helped her produce a record based on the song "Peace Like A River." Fontane hired the Jordonairres to sing backup.

After his conversion to Christianity, Fontane developed a stronger relationship with his brothers, sister and, especially, his father, and made occasional pilgrimages to the Grand Forks mission to sing and speak. At the same time, he suffered significant remorse at how he had treated his parents in his pre-Christian days, and for the remainder of his life rued ridiculing his dying mother and refusing to pray with her. When the Reverend Joseph Trankina died on June 15, 1967, Fontane was crushed.

"As I hurried back to Grand Forks, I was grateful for the times I had with him at the mission during the last few years," Fontane wrote. "One evening, after the funeral as I was making a final check of the mission to be sure everything was in order for the new minister, I heard a knock at the door. It was one of Dad's 'parishioners' who, not knowing Dad had died, had come around for a meal and the evening services.

"I found a can of soup and some bread and prepared them for him," Fontane continued. "As he ate, the man said, 'I never amounted to anything; maybe I never had the right drive, but every time I heard your father preach he made me feel that I was worth something to God. That's important, isn't it?'

"Later, as this man and I worshipped together in the chapel, I realized what a truly abundant life my parents had lived."

Fontane discovered something else during that sad visit. He found that his father, who had earned three doctorates from Lighthouse Bible College at Rockford, Illinois, had served faithfully at the mission for 29 years and had never once drawn a paycheck. The *Kokomo Morning Times*, in a story about Fontane not long after the death of his father, wrote:

"Tears filled the eyes of the man as he remembered the years he had so much, and gave no hand of aid to his father. Fontane says his comfort is in the 'hope and knowledge' that someday he will once again meet his father and mother and say, 'I'm sorry.'"

While Fontane may not have been generous with his father and mother in the days before his conversion, the same could not be said of him toward people in general after he found Christ. One of the most spectacular cases in point occurred in 1964, in Manhattan, as Fontane was walking down Forty-Eighth Street near Eighth Avenue. Elegantly dressed, with an expensive trench coat slung over one of his shoulders and to all appearances not paying any attention to his surroundings, he seemed like a perfect candidate for mugging. At least, one young black man thought so.

The young man raced up behind Fontane and, in one swift, violent movement, yanked the expensive trench coat out of Fontane's fingers, and bolted down the street with it. But instead of reacting impotently, or shouting for help, Fontane took off after him. The chase went on for several blocks, with Fontane steadily gaining ground. Finally, the young man darted into an alley, with Fontane in close pursuit.

Fontane was, by this time in his life, a black belt in karate, so when he came within reach of the mugger, he wasn't at a loss for what to do. He grabbed him, manhandled him, and threw him against the wall of the alley. Looking into Fontane's face, which was wide-eyed and full of wrath, the mugger suddenly began to fear for his life.

"Don't move," ordered Fontane, releasing him.

"Okay, okay," said the mugger. "Take your ----ing coat back."

Fontane grinned, said, "No, no," and then, to the astonishment of the mugger, took off his sport coat, his shirt and his tie, and thrust them into the mugger's hands.

"What the hell are you doing?" he asked.

"If you need the trench coat this much, I want to give you the rest of it, too, because I don't need any of it," said Fontane. "You see, I've got Jesus."

The mugger said, "You're nuts," to which Fontane replied, "Maybe, but just talk to me for a while."

Fontane spent the next forty-five minutes talking with the mugger, whose name was Willie. When it was over, Willie had accepted Christ as his savior. Fontane bought him a plane ticket to Los Angeles, got him a job at the airport there, and remained close friends with him for the remainder of his life.

"When my Dad died, he left all his clothes and jewelry to Willie," said Char. "He was a tough guy, but he had a sensitive side. His heart was made of gold. He literally gave Willie the shirt off his back. I remember him saying to me, 'If anyone ever wants anything, or compliments you two or three times about your clothes or whatever, if the envy is that great, give it to them. It's just a thing. Let them have it and understand the joy you got out of it."

Char also recalled two incidents she witnessed while accompanying her father on a tour of South America. One day, while in a small village in Uruguay, Fontane noticed a girl and her brother begging by the side of the road. He stopped the car in which he, Char and Kerry were riding, and talked to the girl.

"Although she only spoke Spanish, my Dad spoke Italian and there was enough similarity in the languages for him to understand her," Char said. "He learned that the girl and her brother's parents were dead, and that there was no other recourse but to beg. He made housing arrangements for them, and saw to it that they were fed and educated until they were old enough to make it on their own."

On the same tour, in Paraguay, Fontane came across a small beggar boy whose leg had been cut off just below the knee, and wasn't completely healed. The wound was raw, and open, and covered with flies. When Fontane showed concern, the boy said that it was all right – that his parents had "done it to him" so he could make a living as a beggar. Horrified, Fontane whisked the boy away for hospitalization, and then found the boy's parents. He gave them, said Char, "an enormous amount of money" to make sure they and their son would never have to beg again.

"Dad never told anyone about these things," she continued. "Only Mom and I knew. But he did this kind of thing all the time. There are too many instances to list. He really believed that that's what Christ would have him do."

Chapter Eleven

Tony Fontane possessed a keen sense of his own mortality, and he often brooded in private that he would not live very long. While he had developed this viewpoint before his mother's premature death in 1952, it was her passing that convinced him that he, too, would die young. It drove him to excesses of activity, particularly after the 1957 car crash that gave him a new lease on life. He determined to pack as much as he could into whatever time he had left, both professionally and personally.

By 1964, Fontane had recorded twelve very successful albums for RCA and had contributed significantly to improving the religious music market. Lush musical arrangements with big orchestras and evocative new songs, coupled with the lyric tenor voice of Tony Fontane, gave the genre a polish and sophistication it had not known before. Writing about Fontane's album, *Farther Than My Eyes Can See*, a reviewer for *Christian Life* noted that it followed a new pattern in which "the artist is expressing less of self and more love for, and dedication to, the Lord." He commented, also, that "the Tony of today appears to be more relaxed. His voice is less strained, the high notes flow more easily, and, above all there's a softer, warmer tone." This undoubtedly arose from the blending of Fontane's natural ability with RCA's top-notch production values and demanding musical direction.

Burt Lange, Fontane's accompanist in the late 1960s and early 1970s, observed that while the RCA recordings gave full and spectacular play to Fontane's talent, no disc of vinyl could ever truly capture the intricacies of his voice.

"They just don't come through on the recordings he made," Lange said. "Some of his delicate tones could be compared to fine crystal glass. Observing him in person, I could almost imagine that I was seeing the tones of the notes come out and be suspended in air. His pianissimo was out of this world."

American blues and jazz vocalist Ethel Waters also had a personal take on Fontane's singing: "There is a boy with God in his voice, and God can't be in a voice unless He is in the soul first."

Fontane also produced several albums on his own that came nowhere near the artistry and effectiveness of his RCA offerings. Using minimal accompaniment, and with no one to tell him when a song or his singing weren't on track, Fontane knocked out records that were sometimes not up to industry standards and were, essentially, a waste of his resources. But the man felt he had to work, had to share with the world as much as he could while he could, and so he plunged into as many arenas as possible.

Toward that end, Fontane decided to take another leap into movie making. Working again with the irrepressible Billy Zeoli, and casting both Kerry and Char in leading parts, he wrote, starred in, and helped produce a film that would reflect both his unstinted pride in being an American and his dedication to what he called "the star-spangled message of eternal faith and freedom found only in Jesus Christ." The Technicolor documentary tribute to America, *God's Country*, took a year and a half to produce and was released in October of 1964 by Gospel Films.

"Our new film," said Zeoli to the press, "portrays in a graphic way that God created America from strong and spiritually minded men who came from across the world with hearts unthrottled by fear of defeat. They, with hearts aflame, carved from the wilderness this new nation."

While the movie, which portrayed the home life of immigrants as they became United States citizens, was not nearly the global success that *The Tony Fontane Story* had been, it nevertheless received wide play in theaters, churches and auditoriums internationally. Audiences particularly enjoyed hearing Fontane sing "The Battle Hymn of the Republic" and – in a duet with himself as another character – "My Country 'Tis of Thee."

God's Country was successful enough that Fontane made yet a third movie, one that dealt with "the point of no return, when one fails to accept Christ and it is too late." Kerry played the lead in *Christie*, the plot of which involved a nightclub singer who became addicted to heroin, and her struggle toward salvation. Released in 1966, *Christie* may be a lost film. If prints exist, they have not surfaced in many years. *God's Country* also has not been seen in many years, and may also be lost.

As the Vietnam War escalated, so did Fontane's commitment to extending his ministry. Fiercely patriotic and utterly disdainful of men who fled from military service, the World War II veteran made a point to book as many concerts as possible on bases to witness to and show his appreciation for those serving in a time of war. Typical of these concerts was one held at Fort Ord in 1965, chronicled in a newsletter produced by Fontane's office on Hollywood Boulevard.

> Tony spent August 21 at Fort Ord where, in spite of a spinal meningitis epidemic, 1,000 servicemen gathered in the auditorium to hear him sing and give his testimony. Rigid restrictions notwithstanding, these men chose to risk contagion. God wonderfully blessed the service and over 330 decisions were made for Christ that afternoon. One of the soldiers came to Los Angeles a few days later to ask Tony to sing at his wedding.

Lieutenant Colonel Oliver E. Porter, post chaplain at Fort Ord, wrote Fontane a letter of appreciation.

> "It was a personal delight for me to be in attendance and I am certain that my feelings were shared by all who were present," wrote Porter. "In these days of world tensions and military preparations, the men of the United States Army are especially grateful for a spiritual challenge. The effects of your singing and personal testimony for Christ will be a lasting memory for the men."

Also in 1965, Fontane would make the first of four trips to Vietnam to sing for troops serving there. Attendance was always heavy at these concerts and large numbers of men always came forward at the end to give their lives to Christ. The mother of one of these soldiers wrote Fontane:

> "I want to thank you for singing for the soldiers and never compromising our Lord. I received a letter from my

son in Vietnam and he said he had accepted the Lord as his personal Savior at your meeting and that my prayers have been answered. Thank you from my heart and I shall always pray for you, Tony."

Wherever he went in Vietnam, Fontane brought along prints of *The Tony Fontane Story* and *God's Country*, and showed them to his audiences. His newsletter, *Tony Fontane's Record*, reported that "many decisions for Christ" were made at each showing.

Even though Fontane's patriotism was deep and abiding, and his political viewpoints conservative, his understanding of the Vietnam War lessened with the passing years. After his fourth visit to the country – in which his helicopter came under Viet Cong anti-aircraft fire – he admitted to a reporter "knowing less now about the Vietnam situation" than before his initial tour, calling the war a "Ping-Pong game." And yet, he remained one hundred percent in the corner of the American effort and advocated its unconditional victory. "We should win in Vietnam or get out," he said, and lamented the growing unrest in America over the war.

Fontane was not shy about talking to reporters regarding his political views, most of which were wedded to his Christian beliefs. Protestors and liberal politicians were often the targets of these remarks.

On demonstrations in the streets: "Down through history, marches have led to violence," he said. "Those people should use their energy to pray...God ordained ministers to save souls, not march."

On government spending for education and poverty: "Education and poverty programs are not the answer. When you get money, you just want more."

On student takeovers at universities and administrative pandering to them: "I don't want college students running our institutions. They don't have enough experience."

On flag burning and the erosion of patriotism and godliness in America: "When I view those across the nation who desecrate and burn our flag; when I hear so-called leaders in high places compromise on the American spirit and heritage by being willing to accept anything but victory; when prayer and Bible reading are moved from our scholastic system by the highest court in the land, I become greatly stirred to open my mouth and let all know that I love America, and America loves me.

"God," he continued, "is total victory. There is no defeat in God. America's victories, when the odds were always against her, came not merely from our great Army, Navy, Marine Corps, Air Force; not from the hydrogen bombs, or our ability to reach the outer limits of the universe, but our victory always has, and always will come through our spiritual strength."

On February 4, 1965, Fontane was the featured soloist at the White House for the President's Prayer Breakfast. Lyndon B. Johnson was the third of four presidents Fontane would perform for, he having already sung at the White House for Dwight D. Eisenhower and John F. Kennedy. He would also sing for Richard M. Nixon in the coming years. Fontane was allowed to bring a special guest to the breakfast, and he chose to bring his father.

"Tony was elated that he could honor his father in this way by inviting him to be with him on this great occasion," said Nina. "Our Father was thrilled to say the least. He told us that he was deeply moved by the stirring and heart wrenching prayers of these important men. It pleased him to know that leaders of our nation met regularly to seek God for His guidance in their decisions. It made a deep impression on him, one he would never forget."

At the breakfast, Fontane sang two songs – "The Battle Hymn of the Republic" and "The Old Rugged Cross." Vice President Hubert Humphrey was visibly moved during the performance, showing deep emotion during the singing of "The Old Rugged Cross." Humphrey later revealed that it was his father's favorite song and that it had been sung at his funeral.

By 1965, Fontane had been a Christian performer for eight years and had covered more professional territory than any other gospel singer before him. Incredibly, the next eight years

– the last eight years of his life – would see an increase in his professional commitments and achievements, so much that it staggers the mind to ponder the physical, mental and financial cost it all must have had for the singer.

Fontane, who had committed to memory some seven hundred hymns and gospel songs, would, over the next few years, perform multiple concerts in every state in the Union, several times over. He would perform for thirty-one governors. Each year he would appear at two hundred fifty colleges and two hundred high schools, singing a variety of religious and classical music. He performed numerous times for Kathryn Kuhlman's *I Believe In Miracles* television show. He completed multiple tours of Europe, South America and the Near East, all the time mingling his performances with personal testimony and religious conviction. By the end of the 1960s, he was receiving nine hundred invitations a month and traveled more than two hundred thousand miles a year.

"I simply want to improve the world I'm living in," he said of his bone-crushing performance schedule. "Godliness produces results."

Central to his message was that hope for the future lay in young people. It was to them that he frequently directed his concerts and comments. Each year he received more than one hundred thousand letters from "kids in trouble," all of whom he attempted to help through his far-reaching ministry. He noted that less than one percent of teenagers attended church, and it was to these young people he aimed many of his efforts.

"For America's sake, we must help the youth," he said. "If we don't get to the youth, there will not be much of a future for America. It's my belief that America's greatness is in her heritage of Christianity and that if we lose this we will lose the heart of America."

He did take time to be with his family at their Woodland Hills home, but his restlessness often prompted him to pack them up and carry them off to faraway locales. One of the places he loved to visit was the Holy Land. On one of these trips, he made a pilgrimage to the Garden Tomb, which was just a few yards from Golgotha, site of Jesus' crucifixion. It was night, and he was part of a small group of visitors.

"At the request of the caretaker of the tomb, I sang a song for them," Fontane later wrote. "I chose 'I Walked Today Where Jesus Walked' because it was obviously appropriate. But, singing that song at that time and place, it suddenly became more than merely appropriate. It became an experience. And not just for me.

"When I was finished," he continued, "a man came up to me – an American like myself – and said, 'Mr. Fontane, I've been traveling in different parts of the world, going to different places that had an historical interest to me. And that's what this place had – an historical interest. But as you were singing that song I sensed, and found, a stronger interest. Your voice brought me something spiritual.'

" I was deeply pleased, of course, but I knew it wasn't my voice that he had been hearing, it was His voice. And that's why I sing."

For the second time in his life, Fontane was an unqualified success. He had money and fame and a happy marriage. Char, who had steadily worked in television during the 1960s, began to attract the attention of Broadway producers, and was a source of great pride for her father. All seemed right with his world. As reporters Penny Blaker and Ken Francis of the *Kokomo Morning Times* noted in a front-page story about Fontane:

"The ready smiles, the deep, twinkling brown eyes, the youthful glow all proclaim a man who has found 'life.'"

Soon, though, Fontane's world would again come crashing down around him. This time, he would not survive it.

Chapter Twelve

For nearly fifteen years he had lived with pain. Body aches and migraines – reminders of his 1957 car crash – were a constant part of his life. But in 1972 he began to experience new sensations, ones that were unlike anything he had ever felt before. He hurt within his core. There was blood in his urine. His physical relations with Kerry resulted in deep pain, not pleasure. A medical checkup quickly led to consultations with a specialist, who gave Fontane grim news. He had prostate cancer, and immediate radical surgery was recommended. The singer was not yet forty-seven years old.

The surgery that removed Fontane's prostate and the series of painful follow-ups that came afterward were unsuccessful on a number of levels. First, it became apparent that the cancer had spread beyond his prostate and that nothing could be done to arrest it. It was early in 1973 when doctors told him he had about a year to live.

Second, Fontane's career came nearly to a halt as pain and fatigue took their toll on him. He continued to schedule concerts, but soreness and sickness frequently forced him to cancel. There were times, at church appearances in which he knelt with the congregation to pray, that people had to help him to his feet afterward. For Tony Fontane, whose very stationery proclaimed "the world is my concert hall," the world began to contract.

And third, his psyche took a brutal beating.

"Psychologically, the prostate surgery just destroyed him," said his daughter years later. "My dad was very virile, passionate, and all of a sudden that part of his life came to an end. He felt there was some kind of shame in it. My mother spent twenty-four hours a day telling him that it didn't matter to her, that she was just happy to have him in her life, but he would only say to her, 'You don't understand.'"

Char was unaware for some time that her father was dying. He hid the news from her, protecting her as she pursued her very successful acting career and, in March of 1973, prepared to marry a young Italian, Sergio Consani, and move to Italy. Now, as always, he wanted nothing but happiness for his daughter, and didn't want her worrying about him. On March 22, 1973, the day before her wedding, Fontane wrote a poignant letter:

Dearest Char –

Tomorrow is the day you have chosen to take unto yourself a man, Sergio, and to love and live for each other.

There are so many things going through our minds – How wonderful and perfect a lady you have always been. How quickly time has passed since you were given to us by God, and with all of this, we have always wanted the things that were best for you, and those things which would bring you happiness. We want you to be happy now. You are such a beautiful and elegant woman. With your belief and faith in Christ, we know you will find happiness.

We want Sergio to know we care for him, and all we ask is no matter what may arise in life, that he take care of you. You are a rare jewel and we pray he will treasure you.

It will not be as though you are leaving, but merely enroute, for you will always be with us in spirit and in our hearts. Mother has been a perfect wife and help mate and a perfect mother in raising you. If I (Daddy) have failed in any way, please forgive me. Please remember we will always be available to help you and Sergio anyway we can. Our prayers will cover you daily. Thanks for being a truly perfect daughter. We love you, have always loved you, will always love you. You were given to us by God. He always gives the best. All the happiness, joy and success, we pray He will give you.

Now and always –

Mother & Daddy

Four months later, Char was pregnant, and wanted to have her baby in the United States. Fontane offered to fly her home. In September of 1973, she landed in California and was met at the airport by her parents. She immediately noticed that something was wrong.

"My father was almost always happy and jovial, but this time he didn't speak the entire ride home," she said. "I asked him if he was okay, and he answered in a clipped voice, 'Yep, fine.' When we got home, my mother took me aside and told me that he had less than a year to live."

Char didn't want to believe it. God, she said, had saved his life with a miracle once before. God had saved her mother from certain death, as well. He would do the same this time. But Fontane, with his certainty of a brief life, had essentially accepted his fate.

"Why don't you fight this, Dad?" asked Char.

"Because this is the way it's supposed to be," he replied. "I'll be going home soon. Very, very soon."

She asked if he were angry about having his life whisked away just at the height of his success and happiness. He replied, "I'm angry as a human being, that I'm not going to have time to see your child grow, and that kind of thing. But this is my time, Char. It's always been my time."

Char recalled that part of her inability to accept her father's impending death had its roots in personal guilt.

"I really was not a very good daughter," she said. "I was a good girl, but I was not a good daughter. I could have been more loving, and warmer. I will never know what caused me to remain so distant. Looking back on it, I think that I loved him so much that I was afraid if I got too close, something might take him away from me, and the hurt might be irreparable. And that's just what happened."

By 1974, Fontane was so ill that he made only a fraction of the professional commitments he had made in his heyday. It is incredible that he made any at all, given his condition. A lesser man, noted Char, would simply have given up, but not Fontane. He insisted on singing whenever and wherever he could, in order to advance the message of salvation and God's grace. But the physical toll was heavy, and audiences knew by looking at him that he was sick.

Ever since his conversion in 1957, Fontane had promised his father, and God, that he would return to the Grand Forks mission to sing and to minister to the people it served. Now, sick and weak and in desperate pain, Fontane determined to make good on that promise. His sister, Nina, and brother, Joe, eagerly agreed to attend, with Joe acting as master of ceremonies. Excitement grew as word of the concert spread. But in June of 1974, just as Fontane was preparing to make the trip to North Dakota, he took a turn for the worse. Kerry telephoned Nina to say that he was too ill to come, but that she would call back in a few minutes to confirm or deny.

"My son was with me, and we both knelt to pray for Tony," recalled Nina. "We asked God to give him the strength he needed and relief from pain, so that he could come and fulfill his promise to God and our dad.

"A few minutes later," Nina continued, "the phone rang and it was Kerry, saying that if I could arrange to have a doctor and ambulance at the airport, and pain medicine for him, Tony's doctor would authorize his coming. I could do this. We then offered a prayer of thanks to our faithful God."

Nina, who had worked at the Grand Forks hospital for many years as a registered nurse, made the necessary arrangements and took over the medical supervision of her brother at the concert.

"At the concert, you couldn't tell Tony was sick," she said. "He gave his testimony and sang beautifully."

However, at the intermission, Fontane admitted to Nina that the pain was so bad he couldn't continue with the concert. She administered pain medication to him, after which he asked her to go on stage and sing a few songs while the medicine took effect.

"By the time I was finished, he was feeling better and was able to come out and finish the concert," Nina said. "What an ending; he sang his heart out, ending with 'The Lord's Prayer.'"

The mission erupted in a standing ovation.

"Tony had kept his promise to God and to our dad – to return to the mission he once rejected, the place, as a child, he detested," said Nina.

On June 26, 1974, Tony Fontane gave his last performance. He was in a wheelchair, now, too weak to stand alone for any length of time. Char was present at a church in Orange County, California, in which her father was to sing, and watched as two men – one on each side of him – helped him out of the wheelchair and supported him while he sang his final song: "Just As I Am."

"I think he knew that this was it, his last song," she said. "And he sounded great. The voice, that magnificent tenor voice of his, had not suffered at all."

The next day, Fontane suddenly doubled over in severe abdominal pain. He was rushed to West Hills Hospital in Canoga Park, California, where Dr. Harvey Davis quickly diagnosed his condition as "acute hemorrhagic pancreatitis" – a severe rupturing of the blood vessels in the pancreas. In agony, Fontane went into hypovolemic shock, a condition in which the heart is unable to supply enough blood to the body as a result of blood loss.

On Sunday, June 30, 1974, Kerry, Char, and Fontane's two brothers, Vince and Joe, were at his hospital bedside, while his sister, Nina, was on an airplane racing to be with her brother. She was unable to reach him in time. At 9:05 a.m., Fontane – not responding to treatment – suffered multiple organ failure. His family watched as life left the body of one of the greatest Christian voices of all time.

The man who had made a bargain with God, and whose commitment to keeping his side of the bargain had led hundreds of thousands of souls to Christ, now belonged to the ages, and to the God he had served so faithfully.

He was forty-eight years old.

Epilogue

On July 3, 1974, at two in the afternoon, several thousand people jammed the Court of Remembrance at Forest Lawn Memorial Park-Hollywood Hills for the funeral of Tony Fontane. Traffic in the area had to be rerouted, and many who wanted to attend, such as old friend Virginia Simmons of San Jose, California, couldn't get anywhere near the service, which featured an intercom system that played a selection of Fontane's gospel songs.

"I was devastated by his death," Simmons said. "It was such a shock. Most people didn't know he had been sick, and so it was a shock to them, too. At the funeral, we wanted to console Kerry and Char, but we couldn't even get close."

Billy Zeoli was in Switzerland when he heard that Fontane had died.

"It felt like I had lost a part of my body," Zeoli said. "I was with him day and night for so long. We were like brothers. He'd call me up at three in the morning with some stupid story, and there was just nobody else who was that willing to have fun and love the Lord at the same time."

Kerry and Char were consumed with grief – Kerry, of course, because she had lost her husband and soul mate, and Char because she had loved her father so deeply and yet had never let herself demonstrate it.

"I removed myself from him," she said. "He was gone so much that I decided that when he was home, I would be gone from him. I can't describe the remorse I felt, and still feel, over that."

With their grief blinding them, Kerry and Char did something they perhaps should never have contemplated. Some days after Fontane's funeral, they held a "take what you will" gathering at their home in Woodland Hills, in which friends of the family could reminisce about the singer and take small mementos to remember him by. Char said the house was packed with people, not all of whom acted with restraint. They stripped the house of Fontane's belongings, taking away everything including Bibles with Fontane's handwritten notes in the margins, photographs, letters, and even a series of diaries Fontane had kept the last five years of his life. To this day, none of those items have resurfaced. Kerry, said Char, was too numb to either notice or object.

"I, on the other hand, wanted to get rid of everything of my father's that I possibly could get rid of, down to his shoes, because the pain of his loss was so shattering," she said. "The pain was so enormous that I didn't even cry until twelve years after my father's death, and couldn't have a picture of him on display until about 1999.

"Now," she added, "I wish I had all those things back."

After Fontane's death, Kerry embarked on a number of business ventures, including serving as the head of several Barbizon modeling schools. She even returned to acting, in the New York show, *Rhapsody in Blue*, based on the life of composer George Gershwin.

"She walked into the audition, and there were three hundred women there," Char said. "The director took one look at her and said, 'You're the lead.' That's how great she looked."

Kerry toured with the show and enjoyed it, but, as had been the case during her movie career, never took herself too seriously and eventually moved on to other things. In 1988, she accompanied her daughter to Australia, where Char, who was long divorced from Sergio Consani, intended to reside. The Australian press picked up on Kerry's presence in the country, and hailed her as a returning celebrity, recapping in newspaper articles the time she and Fontane had spent touring with David N. Martin and the Tivoli Theatre. Kerry enjoyed the celebrityhood, but admitted to Char that she was lonely, and that she very much missed Tony.

"Just look at you," Char told her. "You're gorgeous. Why don't you get married again?"

Kerry just shook her head and said, "No other man could come up to the standard set by your father. Any other man would be second best."

By the mid 1990s, Char, now retired from acting, was living in Nashville with her new husband, Roy Yeager, drummer with

The Atlanta Rhythm Section. Kerry, who had been traveling with a friend and was planning a trip to Egypt, paid Char a visit. She admitted to not feeling well. Char quickly got her to a doctor, who performed a series of tests. The results were devastating to Char. Her mother had ovarian cancer, and had no more than three months to live.

"I said, 'You're wrong, God can fix this,' which was my answer to everything," Char said. "But my mother knew she was dying. I said, 'Mom, He healed you before,' and she said, 'Yes, but I've been living on borrowed time.'"

Kerry spent most of the last three months of her life at the Nashville home of Char and Roy. Near the end, when her suffering became unbearable, Kerry was admitted to the hospital. Char keenly remembered the last visit to her mother.

"This is it," said Kerry. "I know I'm going to die, now."

"How do you know?" asked Char.

"Because," said Kerry, "your father has passed by this room at least twelve times today. He keeps coming by, and smiling at me."

"When she told me that," Char said, "I knew, too."

That night, on November 20, 1996, Kerry Fontane died. Her body was cremated and her ashes retained in an urn by her daughter.

Char Fontane's life was a blur of activity. As a young woman, she acted in many television shows, including *Barnaby Jones*, *The F.B.I.*, *Love American Style*, *The Love Boat* and *Banyon*, and at one point was a guest star on the popular game show, *Hollywood Squares*. In the 1970s, she starred in a short-lived series, *Joe and Valerie*, with Paul Regina, and was nominated for an Emmy for her role as a young prostitute in the acclaimed ABC mini-series, *Pearl*. Her film credits included *The Punisher*, *Until We Meet Again*, *The Night the Bridge Fell Down* and *Just Enough*, while her stage work saw her snag leading roles in the U.S. tour of *Grease*, *Annie Get Your Gun* and *Bye Bye Birdie*.

Drug dependency, illness, anorexia, and money troubles plagued her throughout her career, which she abandoned in 1989. She established a house-cleaning business and a wedding-events business, both of which she eventually gave up to help her husband produce documentary films. Her world threatened to unravel when she was diagnosed with breast cancer in December of 2003, but a mastectomy saved her life. She began to tell people what God had done for her.

"I have finally found my purpose," she said. "I want to spend every minute I have left on this Earth telling people what He's done for me and what He can do for them. I finally understand what joy really is, and it can only come from knowing and accepting Him and putting Him above all other things in your life...The cancer, you see, was my Christmas gift. And I'm grateful to Him for loving me enough to allow me the chance to walk through that fire."

Char Fontane's cancer would return in just a couple of short years, but in that space of time she never stopped talking to people about God, and about her parents.

"I miss both of them," she told an interviewer. "You don't know what I would give to be able to have an adult conversation with them, just to let them know I'd actually maybe started reaching adulthood."

On April 1, 2007, shortly after moving to Marietta, Georgia, Char Fontane died of breast cancer at the age of fifty-five. She is survived by Roy Yeager and a son from her first marriage, Shaun Fontane.

Today, few physical reminders of the legacy of Tony Fontane exist. None of the many recordings he made for Mercury or Columbia Records have found their way into anthologies of fashionable music of the day, and few people can recall his popular career at all. Likewise, most of his gospel recordings have never been transferred to compact disc and only one or two songs from his RCA days are used in modern compilations of religious or inspirational music. The huge body of work produced by the man seems to have dropped into the maw of time, with the exception of a number of MP3s at Amazon.com. His name recognition among people born too late to appreciate his music is almost nil.

But the records and the television appearances and the fame

he achieved weren't the real contributions of Tony Fontane, although he possessed a healthy ego about them. Rather, the enduring contribution of this man who turned his back on God for the bright lights of Hollywood – and who came back from the brink of death to lead a life of spiritual growth and productivity – is one that exemplifies the grace of God and His power to change lives. Around the world still live untold numbers of people who were affected by his music and his ministry and who credit him with bringing them into the fold of Christianity. Thanks to a car wreck, and a bargain with God, their lives – as was his – were changed forever. We will never know what Tony Fontane might have thought of the direction his legacy eventually would take, but the last few words on his grave marker may give us an idea of just where his priorities lay:

"His mission on Earth fulfilled."

THE END

Tony Fontane Music Available at Amazon.com

The following songs and albums are available as MP3 downloads. Singles from the albums may be purchased individually, if desired.

Popular Career (1945-1957)

Albums

The Popular Songs of Tony Fontane:

"A Love Like Yours"
"All Over Again"
"Bring Back the Thrill"
"Cold, Cold Heart"
"Crazy Heart"
"Friend of Johnny"
"I Still Suits Me"
"I'm Yours To Command"
"Vanity"
"Vision of Bernadette"

Songs By The Fireside With Tony Fontane:

"I Don't Want To Set the World On Fire"
"Two Cigarettes in the Dark"
"Smoke Rings"
"Smoke Gets In Your Eyes"
"My Old Flame"
"While a Cigarette Was Burning"
"I'm Playing With Fire"
"Kiss of Fire"

Singles

"Try A Little Tenderness"
"Gonna Live Till I Die"
"The Syncopated Clock"

Tony Fontane Music Available at Amazon.com

The following songs are available as MP3 downloads.

Gospel Career (1957-1974)

<u>Singles</u>

"His Eye Is On the Sparrow"

"The Lord's Prayer"

"The Holy City"

"My Jesus, I Love Thee"

"Wondrous Word"

"On the Jericho Road"

"Peace Like A River"

"The Lily of the Valley"

"How Great Thou Art"

"Keep On the Firing Line"

Made in the USA
Lexington, KY
09 December 2015